HOW TO MAKE MORE PROFIT

For Doreen who waited nine years
and Margaret who was there when it ended

Also by Michael Lawson

Going for Growth

How to Make More Profit

Michael K Lawson

Gower

Published by
Gower Publishing Limited
Gower House
Croft Road
Aldershot
Hampshire GU11 3HR
England

Gower
Old Post Road
Brookfield
Vermont 05036
USA

British Library Cataloguing in Publication Data
Lawson, Michael
    How to make more profit
    1. Profit 2. Marketing 3. Success in business 4. Business planning
    I. Title
    658.4

    ISBN 0 566 07762 0

Typeset in Palatino by Raven Typesetters, Chester and printed in Great Britain by Biddles Ltd, Guildford

Contents

**PART II   EVERYTHING YOU EVER WANTED TO KNOW
ABOUT MARKETING BUT WERE AFRAID TO ASK**

PART III   UNDER THE MICROSCOPE

Illustrations

Figures

Tables

Acknowledgement

I would like to record my debt of gratitude to Peter Walker and Geoff Taylor for the time they devoted to reading the early drafts of this book and their invaluable suggestions on how to improve it.
The final result is, of course, wholly my own responsibility.

MKL

Introduction: Don't Let Anyone See you Reading This

Before we go any further, take a look around you. Take a good look around you. If you're reading in the bookshop before buying, pull your collar up a little higher and turn your back to the rest of the shop. If you're reading on the beach, lie on your front and look down on to the book. If you're reading on the train, put the book flat down in front of you and don't let anyone see the cover.

I know that when you come across something exciting you want to tell everyone about it. But this time resist the temptation. Above all, don't let the competition know about this book or you will be giving away one of the best competitive advantages to pass through your hands this lifetime. Because today you start following the rainbow. And don't believe what they tell you – there *is* a pot of gold at the end of it and I'm going to show you how to find it.

But before that, let's go back in time a while. Remember when you decided to enter the business world? If you had set up your own business you were going to be Richard Branson . . . or was it Alan Sugar . . . or Anita Roddick? If you went into a corporate environment you were at least going to be John Harvey-Jones or Lord Weinstock.

1

So what happened? Things didn't work out quite as you expected? Or perhaps they did – in which case congratulations. But if you made it big, are you absolutely sure you know *why* you succeeded? And if you didn't, how many times have you yelled at the wall in frustration precisely because you don't know why it didn't work out the way you wanted it to?

Well, by the time you finish this book, you will know why. And what's more, you will know what to do about it.

Somebody is going to make themselves a multi-millionaire after reading this. In fact, several somebodies are going to. The only question you need to answer right now is whether you intend to be one of them. So let's get down to business.

Why this book matters to you

First, a word about how this book is put together and how to read it. The book you're holding is a 'model' of corporate performance. It is a distillation of hundreds of other people's experiences of what makes a business or part of a business work well or work badly. I've put the model together from my eleven years of experience as a management consultant.

Now you may think a management consultant only borrows your watch to tell you the time. But in the last eleven years I've borrowed about three hundred and fifty watches – from Rolexes to the digitals they give away with petrol. I've taken them apart, found out what makes them tick (!) and put them back together again so that they work better.

From working with so many businesses I've found out what makes them succeed and what makes them fail. And my general observation is that most managers of most companies – big or small – don't really *know* what makes them succeed or fail – which is a somewhat sombre thought when you really consider it. I have learned to understand the factors that make for success or failure – and that's what I'm going to pass on to you. If you read on you will find yourself somewhere in these pages. And the light bulbs will start coming on inside your head. But don't stop reading when that happens the first time – because there's plenty more to come.

Earlier I mentioned a 'model'. The purpose of a model is to allow us to generalize from examples and apply the conclusion to a specific situation – your situation. Reading this book will enable you to understand the underlying principles that make a business succeed or fail. And in understanding them you can apply them to your business, whether you're running a 'man and dog' outfit, or whether you're a divisional manager of a big public company or whether you run the big public company *in toto*. And applying the principles means profit – much more profit.

How to read the book

Despite its title, this book is more of a 'perspective' book than a 'how-to, nuts-and-bolts' manual. How you use it depends very much on the kind of person you are. If you tend to operate at a very detailed level, *How to make more profit* will enable you to see your business in a broader perspective – how it functions in the wider environment, how the whole is more than the sum of the parts.

If on the other hand you already operate in this way, you should be able to use this book to become aware of the detailed component parts of the business and recognize the small things that can come up and bite you when you're not looking.

Whichever your perspective let me make a suggestion on how to read the book. When you finish this introduction you should read the rest of the book right through once. By all means make notes on what matters most to you as you go through it. The ideas in this book are not unduly complex – but they are comprehensive. It's important not to get over-involved in one issue. In practice most underperforming businesses (and that's *most* businesses) suffer from problems which are interrelated and you need to appreciate as many of yours as you can.

When you've formed a picture of the general content, go back through the chapters slowly and ask yourself how your own circumstances fit into the model and what you need to do differently. Write down what comes to mind as it comes. You can make it coherent later. And remember – the only people to give this book to are your staff – because they're the ones who will help you succeed even more than you have done so far. Happy reading and call me if you need help (see p. 183).

Structure of the book

I know of only three sets of factors that affect how profitable you are:

1   The external environment in which you trade and which, in all probability, you cannot control to any significant degree.
2   The way you interact with the market environment, i.e. how well you market and sell what you produce.
3   The efficiency and effectiveness with which you undertake or execute the production or work that you do.

If you know of any factors that influence profit but don't fall into one of these three areas, please let me know – I'm always interested to learn more.

Experience tells me that managers often think they have problems in one of these areas, whereas in reality the root cause lies in a different area. If you try to fix what isn't broken in the first place don't be surprised if it makes no difference. First find the real problem, then fix it.

The rest of the book is divided into three parts, each dealing with one of the areas, as follows.

Part I   The big picture
Part I deals with the strategic market environment. Yes, it sounds dull, but don't skip this part. I've often found that it's the failure to understand this subject that prevents a business from performing really well. If you adopt approaches that are wrong for the circumstances you are in you will never optimize performance.

There are two categories of issue in the external environment that affect you – we'll call these economic factors and market factors. Dull though it may be, you need to take an informed view on where the economy is going (and that might be the global, national or regional economy, depending on exactly where and how you do business) to be able to take the right decisions for your business.

As far as the market is concerned, a certain British prime minister once said, 'You can't buck the market'. At least you can't go on doing so indefinitely, particularly if it's a competitive market (and which ones aren't these days?).

You therefore need to be very clear about the most important factors that apply to your market. We'll look at questions such as how mature it is – because the way you make most profit in a mature market is different from how you make it in a developing market. If you're lucky enough to be in an entry-barred market (one that's hard for others to get into) your strategy will be different from what it would be in a highly competitive market – your main aim will be to keep the competition out for as long as possible. So there are all manner of issues that you need to take into consideration here as well. I've already said enough to let you realize that the environment is crucial to your profitability.

Part II   Everything you ever wanted to know about marketing

Part II isn't, of course, everything, but it will look at how you interact with marketing to make the most of your circumstances. Effectively you have two tool boxes – the marketing tool box and the sales tool box.

Marketing deals with how to provide what customers want to buy and how they get to know about it. Selling is how you persuade them to buy. The main issue you need to consider is that the most effective sales and marketing strategies and activities depend on the type of market environment in which your business functions. Select the wrong strategy – the wrong responses to the outside world – and you'll find yourself watching others soar while you plummet. Find the right sales and marketing strategy and you're the one that soars.

Part III   Under the microscope

By the time you've understood the nature of the environment you're competing in and selected winning strategies for making the most of it, you will have business piling up at your door. Nice problem to have, but it *is* a problem. Whether you perform well depends on the effectiveness and efficiency with which you execute the work you generate. And that's why much of this book will be looking at the best way to organize what you actually do. You need to think about a range of factors here from production systems (how you produce, how you hold stock, how you deliver, how you purchase and so on) through resource management systems (people management, IT, financial management etc.) to management systems such as leadership and motivation, and innovation (yes, you'll be innovating by the time you've finished this process).

If you consult any business shelf in the bookshop you'll see dozens of titles on these subjects. Since most of us don't need the wheel reinvented, we'll concentrate in these pages on establishing the key issues in each area and looking at how the various elements interrelate.

The notion of interrelationship is important. Never forget that your business is a system in which everything relates to everything else. Change one element at one end and ripples are created through the whole business. Your business is also a system within a system, because of the way it interrelates with the outside world. React sympathetically to the changes in the bigger system outside and the little systems inside tend to work better.

By the time you reach the end of this book you will have developed an integrated holistic view of your business (you'll also have learned some fancy new terms to impress the dinner guests) and what you can do to make it perform at its absolute best. You'll have opened your own eyes to why you never achieved the results you'd hoped for (or perhaps why you've done so well) and, more important, what to do about it.

Map of the model

As I said in 'How to read the book' above, the purpose of the book is to provide a comprehensive perspective analysis of all the key factors that affect your profitability. There are many factors, but they can be broken down into categories, and each part of the book deals with a different category. To give you a better idea on where we're going, each part of this book begins with a 'Map of the model' that will summarize the factors dealt with. The map of the model for the ground we've covered so far is as follows:

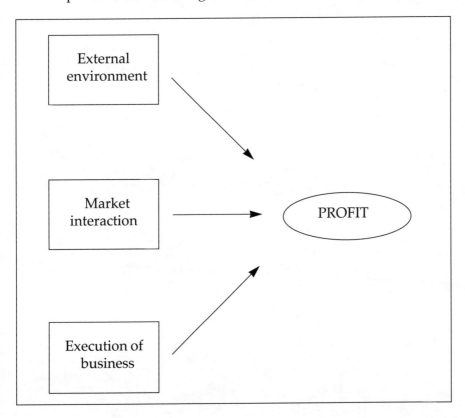

So now let's get down to business – *your* business.

Part I
The Big Picture

It must be remembered that there is nothing more difficult to plan, more doubtful of success, nor more dangerous to manage than the creation of a new system. For the initiator has the enmity of all who would profit by the preservation of the old institution and mere lukewarm defenders in those who would gain by the new ones.

Machiavelli, *The Prince* (1513)

Map of the model

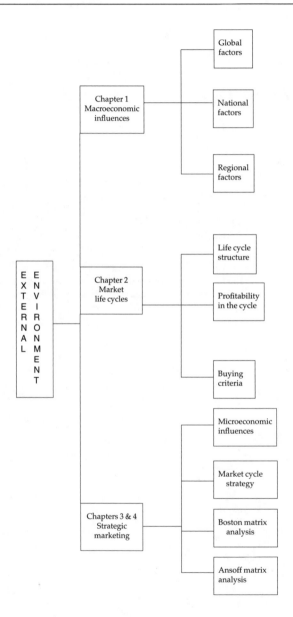

1 Macroeconomic Influences on your Profit

Something I've noticed in business over the years is that managers and owners tend to be quite happy so long as things don't change. When everything rolls along the same way from year to year most people deal quite well with life's little issues. It's when changes happen that the problems start. Quite often people just don't know where to turn next, simply because conditions are different from what they've been used to. And consequently most people seem to regard change as negative – a threat to be afraid of or to be coped with.

If you can reframe that view and regard change as an opportunity rather than a threat, all kinds of possibility begin to arise. You start to see opportunity in every change you face and change itself becomes a friend rather than an enemy.

But regardless of whether you view change as good or bad, what has become more noticeable over the last ten years or so is that the number of changes we face in doing business is increasing exponentially. You can be forgiven for thinking that nothing ever stays the same. Much of this change is technologically driven and we'll be dealing with it in more detail throughout Part I. But here we consider the changes that are taking place and why they are happening.

Maybe if you can begin to grasp what causes change, you can build the expectation of change into the way you manage your business. And that leads directly to looking at the external environment.

Stop and think for a minute about the various groups of factors outside your business that are significant to you. At one level you'll be considering customers, banks and financiers, competitors (although, interestingly, most people don't consider the competition) etc. Jump up a level and you might be inclined to think about public authorities – local government, central government and so on. Jump up another level and start thinking in terms of the macro factors that influence the performance of your business. Those factors can be cultural, political or technological. But they all affect the business world through the media of economies and markets.

Both economies and markets are influenced by the same processes – large numbers of people taking many decisions which together amount to trends. And those trends are what influence the immediate circumstances that your business faces. Naturally, some of the decision-makers are bigger and more influential than others. The bigger the player the more influence their decision might have on you. We see this most obviously in the case of government-imposed changes – say in the rate of VAT. It imposes a change that we cannot ignore – we have to react and charge more VAT. But the same change also influences the environment in which we operate in a more subtle way, affecting the disposable incomes of non-business customers and influencing the choices that they make in relation to your products or services along with thousands of others.

So why does this matter? Simply because if you learn to read trends and processes in the environment you stand a better chance of predicting how the factors consequential to your business will be performing in the future. And if you can do that you can position yourself to take best advantage of future circumstances rather than waiting for them to happen.

The economic environment

A useful place to start thinking about these issues is at the distinction between economy and market. Now in practice an economy is no more than a collection of markets susceptible to the influences of powerful players – especially government agencies. Because those agencies attempt to manipulate economies and because their decisions are mostly rather remote from individual players, in most cases it's best to take economic factors as given, and assume there's nothing you can do to influence them. (There will be exceptions to this, of course, but even the most influential captains of industry that I know tend to have influence over policy relating to specific markets rather than to the economy as a whole.)

Therefore, when considering economic factors from the point of view of your own business, ask yourself these questions:

1 What economic factors are most important to the performance of my business?
2 What is likely to happen to those factors?
3 How should I be acting *now* in anticipation of my conclusions proving correct?

The first question leads to further questions:

1a Does my business benefit cyclically or countercyclically from the economic cycle itself? For example, most discretionary consumer expenditure such as on holidays and cars runs in sympathy with the economic cycle (more are sold when the economy is buoyant) but something like a debt collection service runs countercyclically.
1b Is my business particularly susceptible to changes in one or more specific economic variable? For example, luxury goods expenditure may be particularly responsive to changes in VAT levels, the purchase of holiday homes may be sensitive to changes in capital gains tax.
1c Do I supply discretionary or non-discretionary products/ services? On the whole if customers don't absolutely have to

have what you supply your sales may suffer in economic downturns whereas if your product is a necessity the levels of purchase will tend to be independent of economic activity. For example, most staple food products are likely to be insensitive to levels of economic activity.

Answering these supplementary questions leads naturally to questions 2 and 3:

2   What is likely to happen to those factors?
3   How should I be acting *now* in anticipation of my conclusions proving correct?

Predicting economic change is notoriously difficult so I suggest that the watchword here should be 'flexibility'. But having said that, when was the last time that you assessed the likely prospects for economic factors that are important to your corporate performance? You can sit on the sidelines and simply take the view that it's out of your control, putting yourself on the effect side of the cause and effect relationship. Or you can take the proactive approach which at least gives you a ticket in the lottery.

In this context I suggest that you need to consider three sets of economic factors which may be seen as more or less remote from you:

● Global economic factors
● National economic factors
● Regional economic factors.

Remote in this context doesn't mean that they have no influence on you. It means that the trends affecting you are bigger, the results of many more individual decisions. You might find it helpful to visualize them as in Figure 1.1.

The figure obviously refers to a single-location business that operates primarily in a regional economy. If your business is

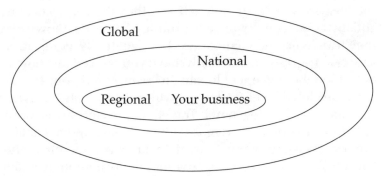

Global

National

Regional   Your business

Figure 1.1   Economic influences on your business

multi-outlet in a given national economy or multinational you position differently according to this factor.

Each level of economic activity has an impact on your business, creating change and opportunity. However, the more remote levels will often make their impact through the nearer levels, and such effects may be consequently less visible.

Global factors

When you think about global factors the temptation is to dismiss them as too remote to be worth considering. But it seems to me that there are some long-term global trends that will have a marked influence on our profit levels and the way in which we manage our businesses. In this context you need to be aware of two key rules of economic activity:

1   If I don't have knowledge/information it cannot influence my decisions. But if I do have, then it will influence my decisions.
2   I will tend to buy from the cheapest source that is commensurate with the service I need (that service includes my required quality level, delivery dates etc.).

Possibly the single most important trend that has occurred at the global level over the last 20 years is the proliferation of information. If I'm used to buying widgets from a given source and don't know about any other sources, I will go on buying from my established source. If you tell me that there's a cheaper, but equally good, equally reliable producer in the next town and that they'll deliver, the chances are I'm eventually going to switch sources of supply (incidentally, have you noticed just how far out of fashion the concept of loyalty in business has gone?).

At the global level, 30 years ago there was much less awareness (i.e. information) in general. Travelling the world was more difficult. Information moved more slowly when it moved at all. Most buying decisions were limited to known and relatively local sources of supply. There is now more information available and my, and everyone else's, buying decisions are made on the basis of that information. Hence rule 1 is obeyed and rule 2 comes into play. My business goes to the cheapest supplier that can meet my quality and delivery requirements.

Stop for a moment and ask yourself 'What is important here for my business?' Well, perhaps for some businesses the superficial answer is 'Nothing at all – I only supply a local market'. So if you run a chain of nursing homes, for example, your service has to be delivered at the point of consumption and there's not a lot that foreign competition can do to match you ... yet.

On the other hand, if you were a motor bike manufacturer in the UK in 1971 you would have found out progressively and very painfully that global trends are crucial to profit and survival itself. UK motorbike production fell from 65,000 units at that date to 3,000 units in 1981 primarily as a result of high-quality low-cost foreign producers entering the market. Similarly, if you're a producer of software in the West in 1996, watch out. There is nothing unique in your production process that prevents it being duplicated by low-cost suppliers in low-wage economies. Equally well trained software writers in India and China can produce for 20 per cent or even 10 per cent of your wage bill. The product can even be supplied almost instantaneously. So long as rules 1 and 2 apply there will continue to be a drift of economic activity towards the low-cost supplier. The Western world has some very difficult decisions ahead of it in this context. And maybe you have, too.

But let's go back to the original line of argument in this section. It's better to have information and an over-view of the big picture which are more likely to put you on the cause side of the cause and effect relationship. The questions you should be asking yourself here are:

1   Am I in a line of activity that is very susceptible to the effects of global economic flows or am I relatively insulated? (Incidentally, my belief is that no one is totally insulated.)
2   If I am very susceptible, what are my options?

Question 2 bears further analysis. Start by defining the nature of the problem. Perhaps you can look at it like this:

Problem: My customers have access to cheaper sources of supply than I am currently providing. They are therefore buying less from me.
Response: Can I reduce my production costs? (See Chapter 9.)
Response: Can I give them significant reason to buy from me despite the price differential? (See Chapters 5–8.)

Note that though these responses are framed for a production business the concepts apply equally well to a service business. In fact they become even more powerful in yielding competitive advantage because the competition is less likely to be thinking in this way.

But if the answer to both these questions is no, you're probably a high-cost supplier in a commodity market (see Chapters 2 and 3) and that really does give you a problem. The only solution left is to produce something different from what you're already producing. That 'something' may be relevant to your existing product range so that it gives existing customers a reason to go on buying from you. Alternatively it may be something totally different to which you can apply your production resources (see Chapter 4).

Whichever way you approach it, it's better to have an idea of where large trends in economic activity are leading because it gives you the option of planning for the future. If you're facing these kinds of issue now, you may like first to examine the range of options in Chapters 9, 5–8 and 2 and 3, referred to above, and then come back and continue reading here.

National factors

Once you have considered the large-scale trends that underlie all economic and market performance, the next natural place to look at is the performance of the national economy. Mature industrial economies (probably all economies) are subject to economic cycles – the ebb and flow of productive and business activity. It's an unfortunate fact of political–economic life that governments try to influence these cycles, ostensibly to smooth them out, but in practice often end up exacerbating them. Hence the resultant boom and bust cycles, recession and depression and all the stuff of economic experience that we have been through in the 1980s and first half of the 1990s.

In this context too, you need to ask some questions:

- What is likely to happen in the foreseeable future?
- How is this likely to affect my profit?
- What can I do about it?

The questions are harder to answer at national level because the future is dotted with potential events that are nothing to do with economics and business – political elections, for example. The best that you can do here is to generate some possible scenarios depending on future events and to plan potential courses of action accordingly.

For example, at the time of writing (Summer 1995) there will be an election in the UK within the next two years. That election will lead either to a Conservative government, a Labour government or a hung parliament. Taking the first two as the most likely possibilities, I need to have an opinion on the likely trend of economic policy in either of these scenarios, and plan accordingly.

My guess would be that in the event of a Labour government we would see higher taxes for high-income individuals, more public spending and more intervention. Under a Conservative government I would expect more privatization, less intervention and lower direct taxes. What matters here is not whether I am right or wrong or whether you agree with me. The important thing is that I have considered the implications of the possible scenarios for my business and I know how I shall act as the picture becomes clearer. You need to do the same. Start by answering the following questions:

1   Are you in a market whose performance is likely to be significantly influenced by government policy?
2   Do you undertake work or sell a product that is in some way publicly funded?
3   Are you dependent on the level of personal disposable income of particular groups or the population as a whole?
4   What contingency plans do you have in place should the level of demand for your product or service change as a result of national economic trends?
5   Which of these potential changes are likely to produce opportunities and which threats? And specifically, what are the opportunities and threats likely to be?

Take for example a client of mine, one of the leading vehicle leasing companies in the UK. Business was booming in the 1980s, along with everyone else's. But the problem with vehicle leasing is that your profitability is fundamentally tied to the residual value of the vehicle when it is returned to you at the end of the lease period. And what happened to residual values in the downturn of the early 1990s? Prices in the second-hand vehicle market plummeted and with them went residual values on the leases. Now, that on its own would be enough strain on the cash flow, but when your balance sheet is mostly composed of assumed residual values, relatively small fluctuations can have a big impact. So it wasn't long before the business was close to technical insolvency and coming under very close scrutiny from the funders. It survived, but only just, and only with some very fancy footwork on the day of reckoning.

Or how about the impact of recession on eating habits? When the 1990s recession first began, the supermarkets noticed an increased demand for pre-prepared gourmet meals. People were evidently eating out less and substituting food purchases for home cooking. The grocery retailers stocked accordingly. As the recession bit deeper, demand for these high value-added products fell and was displaced by demand for food products with a lower value-added component. Yet again, the supermarkets were able to stock according to the impact of national economic trends.

Regional factors

You can keep sliding down the scale as far as you like in considering the importance of economic activity levels to your business – to a given town or community, if it's significant to you. But I usually find that for most businesses, regional levels of economic activity are important – and they do vary.

Remember that different geographical regions specialize in different activities. When the level of activity in an industry is changing, a region that specializes in that activity will be crucially affected. You need only think of shipbuilding on the Tyne or tourism in the West Country to confirm this.

For regional factors, ask the same questions as before:

- What is likely to happen in the foreseeable future?
- How is this likely to affect my profit?
- What can I do about it?

Two things to bear in mind here are whether you are a specialist in the region's specialist area of activity, and whether you supply product/service into a regional economy only. In this context, consider a client of mine in the food business. The company supplied a specialist food product into a regional economy where the consumption of the product was particularly high. Under-capitalized from the start, the business suffered intensely because demand for the product was highly seasonal, depending on the tourist season. The company worked extremely hard for five months each year, making enough to clear the overdraft from the previous low season – only to find that at the end of each high season the overdraft would again start to build up, threatening survival.

After this had happened for a few years the management realized they weren't getting anywhere and decided to seek help.

There were several attendant problems to do with production layout, packaging, information control and so on. On the whole these existed because management was too preoccupied with satisfying demand in the high season and surviving in the low. But the key issue was the cyclicality itself. The solution lay in two areas: an initial injection of funds to cure the fundamental under-capitalization; and a determined push into the markets outside the region in which consumption would not be nearly as cyclical.

It was a great pity that the management was too preoccupied and inflexible to work on stabilizing the business. It went down and was bought out for a song. And the last I heard it was doing rather well for the new parent company that was concentrating on increasing turnover outside the region.

For a great many businesses, particularly small ones, the luxury of choice doesn't exist. If you're a small hotelier in a specific location, to a large extent you're a hostage to fortune as far as economics is concerned. There are, however, ways in which you can insulate yourself financially from the consequences of negative changes in the level of economic activity. If you're in this position Chapter 10 will prove relevant.

However, if you are in a position to insulate yourself from regional economic trends it makes a great deal of sense to do so. Yet again, ask yourself the pivotal questions set out on page 20 and put yourself on the cause side of the cause and effect relationship.

Summary

- Anticipate changes in the big picture and plan your reactions to them before they become a panic-level problem.
- Decide whether you're in the kind of business that is susceptible to global trends in the short term or whether you have the luxury of being influenced only in the long term.
- Recognize if you have a production cost issue on your hands and face sustained competition from lower-cost suppliers in low-wage economies.

- At a national level, identify the main elements of economic policy that most influence your business's performance.
- Consider what you will need to do should those economic variables change over a reasonable planning period.

2 Cycling through your Market

I hope that by this time you're beginning to appreciate the large-scale economic trends that affect your business and realize that you don't have to act as if you're in a turbulent sea without a life-belt. There are things you can do to influence the way the big picture affects you. As the man once said, 'Luck is what happens when preparation meets opportunity'.

It's time now to move down a level and focus on the market in which you actually play. But we're going to do this in two steps. In this chapter we're going to examine some structural and strategic issues relating to what your market is and how it's behaving. In the next chapter we'll look at some specific examples of how to use your knowledge of how the market operates – and what happens if you don't. In Part II we'll discuss some of the other factors that you should consider: customers, competitors and so on. We shall also address the bit most people think comprises the whole of marketing – communication tools and how you interact with your market.

The market life cycle

Once upon a time, in a village very far away, a certain inventor who was keen on cycling found that he kept catching his trousers in the bicycle chain. 'I shall invent cycle clips', he thought. People heard about the wonderful cycle clips and flocked to the inventor's door, clamouring to buy them. The inventor set up in business to satisfy all the demanding people and became wealthy. He bought a racing bicycle and cycled proudly round the village, demonstrating his high-technology solution to the oily trousers problem that had so long plagued his neighbours.

Others eyed the inventor's bicycle enviously and realized that they too could supply bicycle clips and thus become wealthy and buy bicycles. The market grew. Word spread, buyers came from neighbouring villages, and soon producers in those villages set up in production with a view to purchasing bicycles. Eventually every cyclist in the land was buying the product. And the quiet country lanes became increasingly congested with bicycles.

Sadly, the inventor became obsessed with his racing bicycle and gave no thought to improving his product. Another inventor arose who saw a far more effective way of addressing the original need and invented velcro straps for cyclists' trousers. So the cycle clip inventor and his competitors sold less and less. Buyers drifted to the new velcro product manufactured elsewhere and the village once again became a sleepy backwater, known to the world only for its rather fit inventor.

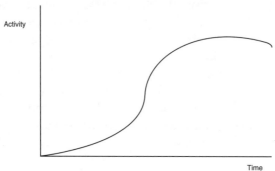

Figure 2.1   Product life cycle

And here, in essence, you have a market life cycle.

A graph of the level of the volume of product sold in the bicycle clips market over a period of time would look something like Figure 2.1.

Bear in mind that the shape and length of the curve will vary from industry to industry, and from product to product. However, most follow an 'S-curve' pattern in some form. The analysis becomes most useful when you divide the life cycle of the product into stages or categories; as in Figure 2.2.

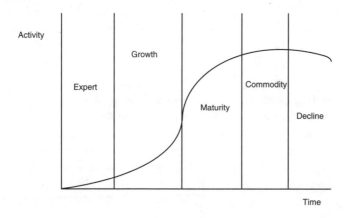

Figure 2.2   Stages in the product life cycle

We can argue until the bicycle tyres wear out about what the appropriate categories are and what shape the curve should actually be for your industry, but the following are the distinctions I find most useful.

Expert phase
You are the only supplier or one of a few suppliers in your market. Your position is preserved for a period from other competitors because of the know-how that you have put into the development of your product. This period will be longer or shorter depending on how difficult it is for other producers to enter the market (the market is 'entry-barred') and how lucrative the potential market is deemed to be by other potential producers.

Lead times for getting into new markets used to be quite long. The technology implicit in many products would often be difficult to analyse and copy and the length of time it took to tool up for competing in the new market was often significant and sometimes prohibitive.

Remember the length of time it took for a market in video rental to become established? For quite some time rental shops were persuading people to buy the first tape for upwards of £40 at 1980 prices. Gradually competition reduced this figure and eventually dispensed with it. But it did take quite a long time.

These days, however, technology itself, speeds of information transfer and increased sophistication in production and management systems have made entry into new markets much faster. Think, for example, of the photograph development market. Time was when you'd send your holiday snaps away or take them to the chemist for processing. You'd wait a week or so and then collect them. Now think about the number of photograph development shops that exist today in most high streets. The march of technology has made the process simple enough and small enough to be supplied direct to the consumer on a retail basis. That can mean one trip instead of two to get your holiday snaps developed, and reduced labour costs are reflected in prices relatively lower than they used to be.

But the implication of ease of access to technology is that, on the whole, if *you* can supply a service then so can *I*. If a photograph development machine is available to you then it's also available to me. The result of this is that more and more markets become easier and easier to enter (so long as capital is available) and competitive advantage is shorter and shorter lived. In most consumer markets major product developments are said to offer time advantage of perhaps only six months before the competition, who are usually equally well placed, catch up.

The distinguishing characteristic of the expert phase in any market is that it usually yields high unit profit for low volume. This means that producers will sell relatively low volumes of product initially but at relatively high prices. The phenomenon is easiest to observe in high-technology markets. Digital watches and infra-red remote control products are good examples.

Remember the time when people used to press a button on their watches to get a red display? You knew they'd spent a fortune on the watch and relatively few people had one. Not too many years later the same product was being given away at the petrol stations and everyone had one.

The significance for you is that if you are in the expert phase of your market you need to understand the profit characteristics of the phase as well as what is likely to happen as the market moves up the curve. If you act appropriately you can take best advantage of the situation. More on this later.

Growth phase

Eventually other suppliers enter the game and the market enters the growth phase. At this stage it can feel that you're doing everything right and you've reached the pot of gold at the end of the rainbow.

My observation is that business managers and owners at this stage of the cycle often feel that they can't put a foot wrong and that they are personally responsible for the success and growth their businesses are achieving. Profits are rising, growth prospects are excellent and all the executive toys seem like only a minor indulgence. After all, what can possibly go wrong when you're growing at N per cent a year and you're personally talented enough to go on doing so for ever? In short, people grow complacent. But at this point take a great deal of care. The maturity phase is only a short time away.

There are actions you should be taking now to ensure your longer-term survival and prosperity. No one's saying 'don't have the toys!' Just understand what the market is doing and don't take your eye off the ball. The expert and growth phases are temporary windows of opportunity. During this time you should be preparing for the more demanding later phases. We'll come back to what that means in practice shortly.

Maturity phase

At some time the chances are that the shine is going to wear off this wonderful growth that you've been clever enough to generate. Eventually you realize that, whilst things are still just about

OK, the rate of growth is somehow not what it used to be. Customers are still phoning you but maybe not as often as they were last year. Star salespeople are still earning big bonuses, but the cheques aren't quite what they were and maybe they're working much longer hours to achieve their targets. If you recognize this, you've probably been through a maturity phase in your market.

By my definition this takes place just as the life cycle curve turns from concave to convex. The big difference is that the rate of growth is slowing and it's a sure sign that in due course you will enter the next phase.

Commodity phase

Why 'commodity'? I would define a commodity as a product or service which I, the customer, perceive to be materially identical regardless of the source from which I purchase it. Of course, nothing is ever fully identical and most producers would be incensed to think that there was no difference between their excellent product and the competition's inferior stuff.

If you're to understand this concept properly you have to see it from the customer's point of view, not the supplier's. Your door chime may play 'Land of Hope and Glory' and your nearest competitor's may play a musically inferior 'God Save the Queen', but if I as the customer don't regard that as a significant distinction then as far as I'm concerned the two products are effectively identical, i.e. there is no material distinction between them. And if there's no difference, what determines my purchase choice?

Well, on the whole there are only three key buying criteria in a commodity market:

- Price
- Availability
- Service.

These are the areas in which you have to compete if you are operating in a commodity market. Of course, you can take the view that the customer is non-discerning or just plain stupid to fail to notice the superiority of your service. But whatever you think of him he is still the customer and he exercises buyer's choice. More on this later.

Before we move on, there's one further point I'd like to make here. I suggest that more and more of the world's markets are tending increasingly towards commodity status as each year goes by. Many if not most world markets seem now in over-supply, and customer choice has proliferated. My expectation is that more and more of us will have to become used to operating in commodity markets. For that reason we'll be paying special attention to the characteristics of commodity markets and what you can do if you are in one.

Decline phase

Some markets never seem to reach a decline phase, or if they do so the decline is very long and gentle (matches, for example?). This may be because the products are a staple necessity for the life we lead and will continue to be so for the foreseeable future. Or it may be because players in the market are able to innovate. In practice this means they can continue to improve the product and so create a new growth phase for the market, as in Figure 2.3.

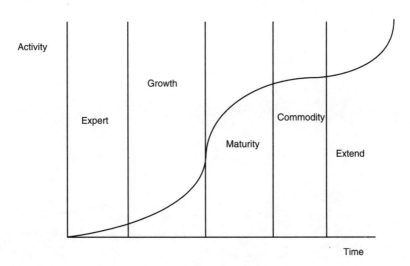

Figure 2.3   Extending the market life cycle

This trend is particularly evident in high-technology markets such as personal computers. The next release of the software, or the next enhancement of the hardware, serves perpetually to impose extensions on the market life cycle. If this doesn't happen, the market will at some point go into decline. This is not a good time to be heavily dependent on such a market for your livelihood.

One further point for theoretical purists: all these events happen against the background of the economic cycles identified in Chapter 1, which can make trends hard to detect. For example a market may appear to be in decline when you might expect it to be growing, or it might revive after a period of decline. To obtain accurate data on this you would have to compensate mathematically for the peaks and troughs of the economy's cycle so as to be able to observe the market's own cycle (anybody got a spare statistician they can lend me?). However, for those of us on planet Earth I suggest it's an acceptable working approximation simply to be aware that the life cycle is operating in your market and act accordingly.

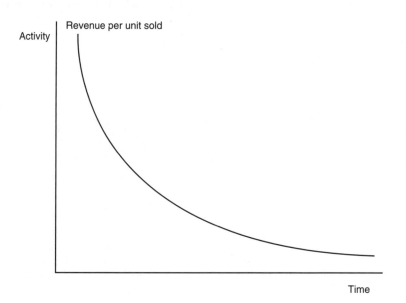

Figure 2.4   Unit revenue/profit over the life cycle

Question: how come the market life cycle is so important to you? Answer: because your position on the curve fundamentally affects two things: how you should be competing; and how much profit you are making. The next chapter discusses competition. But for now, why does the position on the curve affect profit? Think about it in this way. In the early stage of the market you are selling relatively few items but making a relatively high profit per item. As the market grows, the volume you sell increases but the price or profit per item drops. Thus a graph of profit or revenue per item over the life cycle would look as in Figure 2.4.

Now, think about the total revenue you earn on all the units you sell. In the early part of the curve a few units are sold at a high price. At the other end of the curve you sell a great many units but at a very low price or profit margin. Both positions give you relatively low profits compared to the mid-point on the curve where you sell quite a large number of items, but at a relatively high price. If we now add this to the graph it appears as in Figure 2.5.

The crucial conclusion to draw from this is that the best place to be on the life cycle curve is usually in the growth and maturity phases. And just remember how it feels to be there – everything is going well and apparently set to continue to do so for ever. So, the questions you should be asking yourself at this point are:

1 Exactly where on my product's life cycle curve do I think I am at present?
2 How can I spend as much time as possible in the growth and maturity phase where the profits are generally at their best?

In essence, I can see two ways of maximizing your time at the growth and maturity phases. First, find a way of extending the growth phase as in Figure 2.3. Second, cease involvement with this product at or before it moves into commodity phase and move into another product that is in the growth phase.

Extending the growth phase
There are three ways to extend the growth phase as far as your own business is concerned:

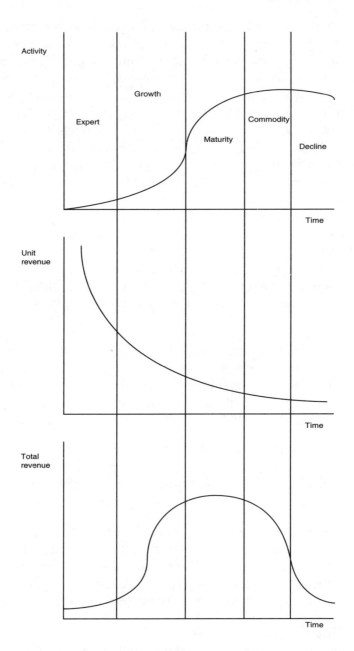

Figure 2.5   Total revenue/profit over the life cycle

1 Find a genuine improvement to the current specification of the product which will attract further buyers into the market (see the case study in Chapter 3 for an example of how to do this).
2 Achieve brand dominance and keep bringing out 'new improved' widgets which persuade customers to buy more.
3 Concentrate on a niche market.

In many respects, the first of these is the best option because it's good for you, good for your customers and good for all of us. Unfortunately, it's not always the most practical route due to the difficulty of finding genuine product improvements in some markets.

The second option doesn't appeal to me as I'd rather be supplying products and services that are genuinely enhancing to the customer and his/her lifestyle or business. Nevertheless, multi-million pound businesses are built on branding and rebranding what is largely the same product (ever wondered why we have so many soap powder brands from so few suppliers?).

The third is a common route forward. Fundamentally, it amounts to concentrating on a small part of the market ('segmenting' the market, to use jargon). The logic is that if you can't grow your turnover and market share in the whole of the market you may be able to achieve much the same result by doing it in a segment of the market.

A good example of this is the way the replacement window industry has functioned over the last 20 years. In the 1970s many of the houses built between 1930 and 1950 needed replacement windows. Some bright individual lit on the idea of aluminium as a better material for replacement windows because of its length of life. Later, it was largely supplanted by UPVC. The market grew and fortunes were made. Most companies undertook almost the whole production process. They would buy in UPVC extrusion, glass and all the other components, make the windows, sell them and install them.

But as the market went through its growth and maturity phase more and more suppliers entered the arena because it looked lucrative. This eventually brought it to commodity status and profit margins dropped. Suppliers' profit and growth aspirations could not be satisfied and they looked for new ways of making and growing profit.

Some left the market and went on to do other things. Many chose instead to concentrate on one part of the process (to 'niche' market), became more specialized and grew profit and market share in parts of the production process. Increasingly we see companies in this industry specializing in frame manufacture, glazed unit production or sales and installation.

Specialization leads initially to higher profitability than could be achieved by addressing the whole of the production process. In turn greater concentration on particular parts of the process allowed suppliers to produce higher volumes and as a result cut costs. Lower costs in the competitive market have led to further price competition. Thus continues this rather elegant dance, with ever increasing efficiency leading to lower costs and competition, leading in turn to lower prices.

Elegant perhaps it is, to the disinterested observer. But if you're on the inside of an industry where this is happening it's a real headache. The very nature of competition means you have to find more ways of cutting your prices each year. So is there an alternative?

The alternative
What if there is no realistic way to extend the growth phase for your company? What if you've come to the end of niche marketing and the ability to save on costs? Well, if you catch this early enough there is often an alternative. As we'll see in the next chapter in more detail, one of the features of the maturity and commodity phases is that suppliers often try to buy market share if they can't grow it generically. You might consider whether selling out is a viable alternative.

Perversely, however, the very time when it may be best to sell (in view of a coming commodity market with low profitability) is often the time when you feel least inclined to do so. Remember the feelings mentioned earlier? The growth phase is typically characterized by an unrealistic euphoria that goes hand in hand with a feeling that what you're achieving is due to how clever you are and has nothing to do with forces beyond your control. As you enter the maturity phase, you see that the growth rate isn't quite what it was, but it's bound to recover – or so you think. The problem is that you don't feel inclined to get out of the market at this point even though there may be opportunities to do so. Most people then let things ride until the commodity phase when profitability has dropped and the price at which they can sell out has dropped with it – if they can sell out at all.

Let's face it. To do well in business requires cool realism and an awareness of what may happen in the future as well as what is happening now. Coming out on top often means having the courage to do the opposite of what everyone else is telling you. You should therefore consider the following: Are you in the maturity phase? Is the commodity phase coming? Should you be getting out while you can? Unfortunately there are no certainties in all this. But an awareness of how markets work might help you make the right decision this year. Next year it may well be too late.

How all this works in practice

You may still be asking what the relevance of all this is to you. Let me quote an example of what happens if you don't pay attention to the life cycle of your product. I have had the opportunity to observe a particular business as it passed through all the above phases over the last 25 years.

A certain entrepreneur set up in business at a time when his industry (the photocopier market) had been ambling along in a steady-state commodity phase for more years than anyone could remember (it was back in the days when folk didn't apply quite such rigorous analysis to the marketplace as they do now because there were plenty of opportunities to make profit). The entrepreneur was well financed and hard-working but he was also fortunate in that he was entering the market just at the time when it was about to undertake very significant growth. Alterations in work styles meant that more of the product would be in demand than had been the case in the past and variations on the basic product would proliferate over the coming few years (remember the bit about segmentation and niche marketing above).

The business was quickly established, the company made good profits and the inevitable fast car and fancy lifestyle arrived – though not at the expense of financing the business and not that I've got anything against fast cars and fancy lifestyles. The only problem I could see was that the entrepreneur was totally convinced that the success he was achieving was due to his personal brilliance. He simply took no account of market forces and the impact they were having on his opportunities for creating a successful business.

The company grew and grew. It eventually floated on the London Stock Exchange in a blaze of publicity – just as the market was shifting into commodity status where profits would become harder to make. As the market became tighter and tighter, the company (having floated) was under pressure to produce better and better results each year. And to do so they had to take increasingly desperate measures. On one occasion one of those measures took the company too far and killed it.

To give the entrepreneur his due, he immediately sought to start again. But it's infinitely more difficult to establish a business in a commodity market than in a high-growth market.

Don't let the same thing happen to you. Be aware of market phase characteristics and what you can do about them. And it's to this subject we turn in the next chapter.

Summary

- All markets go through life cycles. Those life cycles can be depicted graphically by measuring levels of sales over time.
- The curve so depicted will often be S-shaped, but will vary in practice from industry to industry.
- The life cycle of the market can be divided into distinct phases: expert, growth, mature and commodity.
- The opportunity to earn profits varies from phase to phase but is typically at its best in the growth and maturity phases.

- This should lead you to concentrate on spending as much time as possible in the growth and maturity phases of the markets you address, perhaps by product improvement, brand awareness or concentration on niche marketing.
- The rate at which markets move along the curve depends on the ease or difficulty with which suppliers can enter the market and the rate at which demand for the product grows.
- Nowadays, equal access to technology often means that markets are relatively easy to enter for organizations large enough to bear the capital costs of entry.
- The apparently insatiable hunger of suppliers for growth is increasingly resulting in more and more world markets and local markets being in continuing over-supply or commodity market status.
- This in turn has implications for the buying criteria used by customers, who increasingly buy according to price, availability and service.

Key characteristics of each phase of the market are set out at the end of Chapter 3.

3 Some Things you should know about Strategic Marketing

In the last chapter we identified the phases of the market life cycle for most products and services. If you've been applying all this to your own market you will by now have a fair idea of where on the life cycle curve you find yourself.

We also stressed that people tend to behave in very different ways depending on the stage of the life cycle they have reached. That behaviour is often largely driven by an instinctive response to the immediate circumstances, in ignorance of how the market is going to develop. I've already intimated that if you can step back to look at the big picture of market development you will be able to gain a broader perspective that will allow you to decide more thoughtfully how to behave in your market – or more specifically how to compete and position your business.

I'm assuming that the aim is to make maximum profit over the long term. Any fool can make maximum profit in the short term. The clever bit is to *sustain* your profit-making position and capacity. It may already be evident to you that the way to do this varies depending on your place on the life cycle curve.

To understand how best to position yourself in any phase of the market it's important to understand how the market moves from one phase to another. And to do that we need to delve briefly into microeconomic theory.

How microeconomics fits in

I've already referred to the concept of entry-barred markets, which relates to how easy or difficult it is to enter a particular market. All that follows assumes that reasonably free entry into the market is possible. If you're already active in an entry-barred market, congratulations – we'll come to you a little later on. But for now let's concentrate on easy-entry markets.

One of the first things they teach you in microeconomics is a theoretical construct called the 'perfect market'. Such a market must meet certain conditions, for example:

- large numbers of buyers and sellers;
- no disproportionate ability to influence the market on the part of any player (i.e. no 'market power');
- equal access to information.

The theory suggests that under those conditions there is free entry into and exit out of the market on the part of all players. Their presence or absence is determined by the attractiveness of the prices being struck. This in turn is determined by the balance of supply and demand in the market at any one time. Typically, the faster the market is growing (fast growth is usually an early-stage phenomenon) the higher the level of demand, relative to the level of supply. This in turn makes for relatively high profits which attract new suppliers into the market. Their entry is restricted only by barriers to entry. If these do not exist or are relatively low, suppliers enter the market fast. Eventually, the theory goes, so many suppliers will be attracted into a market that, with increased competition, profit will fall to a minimum acceptable level known as 'normal profit' (of course, no one's ever willing to define exactly what normal profit is!).

If you had asked economists for an example of a perfect market years ago they would have mumbled a bit and finally come up with the stock market as the nearest example they could find. Of course, since the advent of screen-based trading and the speed of information flows that implies, the stock market is even closer to the perfect model now than ever before.

So what does this have to do with our line of reasoning about market life cycles? Well, I would simply suggest that the further up the curve a market moves towards commodity status, the nearer it is moving to the theoretical construct of the economist's perfect market. And more and more of the markets that we play in are moving ever closer to perfect competition as information becomes more easily available.

The importance of all this to you and your business is that the things you need to do to maximize profit at any stage of the life cycle curve depend critically on your understanding that your market is moving inexorably closer to commodity (or perfect market) status.

Think about it. Remember when you were in an expert market. You thought your skill was a black art that no one else would ever understand and that the customers would always flock to the door. You were making superb profits and enjoying every minute of watching competitors trying in vain to enter your market. You kept your prices high and gave no thought to marketing. After all, why spend money on business generation if you're the only feasible supplier? Business will be good for ever, so let's enjoy it.

And then one or two competitors began to produce what you produce. Well, it was a bit of a bruise to the ego, but not really important. Their products were inferior anyhow and there were still enough customers to go round, weren't there?

In fact, the problem only really began to come to light a bit later when a large number of suppliers began to join in, and customers had more choice. It was only then that you really had to think about modifying your behaviour to take account of what everyone else was doing. But by that time it was too late. You'd lost control of the market and you were only one among many similar suppliers.

So go on – admit it. What would you have done differently if you had your time over again? Specifically, what would you have done if you knew the market would progressively open up to other suppliers? If you'd had any sense you'd have acted to preserve your position before and as it happened. You'd have done everything in your power to discourage competition. You'd also have made very sure that as competition arose as many customers as possible still preferred to buy from you.

To put it into economists' terms, you'd have done everything in your power to sustain the *imperfections* in the market that were keeping others out when you started. You'd have created or supported as many barriers to entry as you possibly could. In marketing terms, you'd have done anything you could to sustain your competitive advantages for as long as possible.

This all leads inexorably to a set of behaviours that you should consider adopting at each stage of the market life cycle, depending on how influential you are in the market. We turn to this next.

How it works in practice

The best way I can illustrate what to do and what not to do is to give an example of a particular organization (which we'll call company A) that was a subsidiary of a very substantial international conglomerate. This particular company was a UK-based business – an importer of a microelectronic product that was important in manufacturing industry. The company had had several owners over the years, and indeed, if you went back far enough it was actually credited with the invention of the product.

Some ten years before our respective paths crossed they had had a market share in excess of 20 per cent of the UK market and there were perhaps half a dozen other significant suppliers in the market. By the time we met their market share had fallen to around 5 per cent and there were over 20 suppliers – and nobody knew why it had happened or what to do about it. No prizes for guessing the nature of the assignment: 'Tell us why, tell us what's gone wrong and tell us what to do about it.'

Well, the market life cycle seemed a good place to start, so we began to look at the growth rates and numbers of suppliers that were evident over the ten years in question. Sure enough, the market appeared to be going through a traditional S-curve growth pattern that is so easily visible in high-technology industries. But this company had been fiddling while Rome had been burning.

The expert phase

Having virtually invented the product, the company sat back and enjoyed the fruits of its intellectual labour. Certainly, it had put sales people on the road but no serious attention had been paid to brand development until the company began to feel the pressure from other suppliers.

The growth phase

While company A had been reaping profits a particular competitor (which we'll call company B), a subsidiary of another international conglomerate, had been taking a different view. They understood from the beginning that technological advantage was short-lived and they had built their business firmly with the intention of winning and maintaining market share dominance.

As it happened, in the early stages of the market each of the competing products ran on different software languages. That meant that customers needed specifically trained engineers for each version of the product installed in the factory. Naturally, they tended to buy the product from a single or at most a dual source because training the engineers was expensive. And more important, once the decision had been made to source from a particular supplier, there was considerable reluctance to change to another because it would mean changing all units of the product in a given plant (since the technologies were incompatible) and retraining or replacing the engineers. Clearly, that first purchase decision was the crucial one. Company B invested heavily in brand identity and in achieving sales volume, even when that meant lower margins than might have otherwise been achieved.

While this was going on, company A was congratulating itself with the knowledge that they were unlikely to lose their existing customers due to the inflexibility of the technology. They had deliberately positioned themselves as a high-quality supplier to international purchasers and devoted little or no attention to the expanding middle market. In fact, they saw their key competitive advantage as being the robustness of their product which had to operate in a hostile physical environment. This was a viable position when the price of the product was high and the cost of replacement or carrying spares was significant, but became a problem later.

Markets move on. And this one followed a fairly common pattern over the next few years. As the price of technology fell steadily more smaller customers entered the market. They were still largely ignored by company A, but company B, by deploying a large sales force and a high branding profile, picked up the major share of the emerging market.

The mature phase
Company A began to find itself under pressure. As is common in high-technology supply, they found that as the price dropped they needed to sell more and more volume to sustain a given level of turnover. This was fine until their 'quality' customer base reached saturation level: they had bought all the product they needed for their factories other than on the replacement cycle – and that could take 20 years. Company A started to survey the market to see where they could go next but found that wherever they turned company B had been there already. Company B's brand identity was well established and it had a leading, if not dominant, market share. In addition, their product consistently sold for less than company A's. Company A was snookered and each year saw its market share drop as it was marginalized in the high-quality, high-price niche that had seemed so attractive just a few years before. And as the price dropped, the physical robustness of the product seemed less and less relevant, as replacement costs dropped accordingiy. Company A was focusing on a competitive advantage that even its own customers viewed as decreasingly relevant.

The commodity phase
About the time we were working on the exercise company B

dropped a bombshell. Everyone knew that the product price was falling steadily and what had cost £5000 a few years before was now down to about £750. Company B then took the whole market by surprise by introducing a version of the product that retailed at just under £100. This strategically brilliant step opened up even the smallest factories to the benefit of introducing the product into the production process. Furthermore the software and connections essential to functioning were integrated into the product. Added to this, customers now understood the software well. The result was a significant decline in customer inertia.

Company B had thus created a mass market for the product almost overnight. Hand in hand with this went a new distribution strategy. With a pricing structure like this you simply cannot afford to supply direct and maintain a large sales force – you have to sell off-the-shelf through an independent distributor network. And guess who had already tied up the best-placed distributors throughout the country?

In this way company B secured an even larger market share and was now positioned to sustain high volume and high total margin. The outlook for company A was not too hopeful on the face of it. Table 3.1 summarizes the situation. Consultants are not engaged to tell you what your problems are – you normally know those already. The question was what to do about them.

It was quite clear that company A had an unsustainable position in the market as things stood. Niche positioning on high price/high quality was looking more and more like the wrong decision. It was also clear that company B was going to be the dominant force in the market – company A had lost market leadership for good. But the one ray of hope was that the other key suppliers – about six or eight of them – didn't seem to know much more than company A about what was going on – Company B had caught the whole industry by surprise.

After much discussion the strategy that eventually emerged was a progressive repositioning of the business. Company A would introduce its own commodity product. It could only do this by growing its market share. But the new low-end market was still emerging and, apart from funding the required investment, the only real barrier to entry was establishing the

Table 3.1   Behaviour of companies A and B through the life cycle

Life cycle phase	What B did	What A did
Expert	Realized that they had a window of opportunity and that others would enter the market.	Did not realize.
	Invested in technology to keep the product well ahead.	Invested in technology to keep the product well ahead.
	Made substantial reinvestments of profit in building identity and market share.	Distributed the bulk of profits to the parent company and made almost no play for market share maintenance.
Growth	Invested in branding and market awareness to make it as difficult as possible for the competition to enter the market.	Had no awareness of the importance of investment in the market as opposed to the product itself.
	Smothered the market with sales staff to lock new buyers into B as supplier.	Maintained a minimum sales force to serve the needs of the tied customer base.

		Did not seriously seek to extend the customer base into medium sized customers.
Mature	Drove costs down as fast as possible to sustain market share at a dominant level and make it difficult for competitors.	Niche-positioned as a high-quality high-cost supplier; this became increasingly unsustainable as the market moved to high volume and low price.
Commodity	Established distribution channels appropriate to a mass market –high-volume/low-value sales and locked in the best distributors.	Sustained direct distribution and sales strategy more appropriate to a high-price/low-volume environment. By the time they saw the need for distributors the best ones were gone.

distribution network. Company A had to find a way of increasing market share, increase its brand awareness and establish a distribution network. All this was feasible but expensive. After much persuasion company A's parent agreed that considerable investment in the brand was going to be needed to re-establish a viable market position and made the necessary funding available. A distribution network was established (not the best sites, but there were still some reasonable ones left) to carry a new commodity-level product and an intensive brand awareness campaign was mounted that was to run for over two years.

The net result was that company A rebuilt its market share from 5–6 per cent to around 9 per cent in two to three years, all at the expense of the other players – but not company B who were far too cute to let go of the position they had established.

The moral of the story is that company A could have done everything that company B did and could have done so more easily and cheaply in the early stages of the market. If the strategic nature of what was going on had been understood the result might have been very different.

Strategic positioning through the life cycle

The purpose of the example in the last section is to encourage you to reconsider how you should be positioning yourself competitively at the various stages of the market life cycle. At the beginning of the chapter we referred to the fact that in the absence of awareness of how the market will develop, suppliers tend to react only to immediate circumstances, or worse still, believe that nothing will ever happen that they can't deal with. If you're wise enough to be seeking something more than this happy-go-lucky approach, what should you be doing?

The expert phase
Let's start by assuming that you're the first or one of the first to enter a new market. The questions to ask are:

1   Is the market attractive enough for competitors to want to enter?
2   Precisely what is keeping them out at the moment? In the vast majority of cases the answer to question 1 will be yes. The answer to question 2 may be that you have technology that others lack, not necessarily technology in the IT sense, but perhaps skill-driven. However, in most organizations your advantage is likely to be IT or intellectual property, either of which can normally be duplicated eventually. Or the barrier may be market-driven –

you're already so well positioned in the customers' eyes as the supplier of this particular product that no one else can touch you. However, this is only likely if you've already established your market reputation -- your new product is merely an extension of an existing market. Or there could be structural factors that are keeping others out such as regulations, patents, copyrights or official monopolies.

Assuming that your profits are high enough to make competitors want to enter the market if they could, the nature and longevity of those barriers to entry is crucial. If they are going to be long-lived, you have time to play with. You may be able to afford a high-price strategy for a time because there is nothing that others can do to get in. But be careful not to end up with a reputation amongst customers as a malevolent supplier or they may desert you in droves when others finally do enter the market. Of course, this begs the question of how you would know your customers' opinions of you in these circumstances. For more information on this see Chapter 5.

A better strategy may very well be to use the time you have available to take alternative action:

- Develop the technology that is keeping others out to the next level so as to maintain your technological advantage.
- Establish your identity with the customer as the only credible source of supply for your particular product or service.
- Concentrate on adding so much value to the core product with each enhancement that it is simply too difficult for others to compete.

These are the options available if you want to maintain barriers to entry. And we can usefully characterize them as technological solutions or marketing solutions. Put another way, either what you do or offer *is* better or the customer *perceives* it to be better. Of course, ideally, it's both. Either way, I suggest that the best strategy for the expert phase is to maintain barriers to entry for as long as you can.

The growth phase

At some point, unless there are good reasons to prevent it, the market will move into the growth phase. We can usefully define this as happening when a significant number of suppliers enter the market. You will define 'significant' in your own way, of course.

The most noticeable characteristic of the market at this stage is that good profits are still available and you'll be tempted to ignore what is happening. But beware – this state of affairs will not continue for ever. From here on, you need to be aware that the market is marching steadily towards commodity status. So, what is the most appropriate competitive positioning?

First. I expect that margins, though still good, are less attractive than they were in the expert phase. You'll be tempted to try to maintain them above the competition or alternatively to cut them more than necessary. Either way, I suggest that you need to be keenly aware of what the competition is doing – and very few companies that I know pay adequate attention to this. We'll look more closely at competitor analysis in Chapter 8.

If new players are entering the market, your share of it is almost certainly falling. That's probably not important to you now because profits are still good. But it will be crucial as the market moves to the next phase. Consequently the most advantageous strategy at this stage is likely to be to play for market share. You do this by developing your product and correctly combining all the marketing communication tools available to you. Chapter 5 deals with this. You can't continue to be the sole supplier in the market, but you may be able to remain the leader or dominant player. However, if you don't get the market share issues right in this phase of the market it's going to be very expensive to recover lost market share later.

The mature phase

At this stage of the market the competition is beginning to increase. Almost perversely, existing players often aspire to high growth rates just at the time when the intrinsic rate of growth in the market is beginning to fall back. It's almost as if players have needed the growth phase to build their confidence in their own ability to grow in this particular market. Perhaps several years of, say, 10 per cent growth leads them to target 15 per cent next year. And just when they have the confidence to aspire to increase their growth rate, the market begins to level off.

If you want to grow your business faster than the market is growing, the only way to do so is to take market share off someone else. At this point suppliers' strategies can become aggressive – price wars start, deep discounting takes place and big money is thrown at brand awareness campaigns.

Consider how much easier it would have been if you'd thought about maintenance or growth of market share in the earlier market phases, when the market was still growing fast enough to satisfy everyone's aspirations. What would have happened if you'd established high levels of customer service and investment in technological development and in brand maintenance at that time? But most players don't think about these issues until they're failing to get the growth they want. So how do you do it now you're in the mature phase? Well, you could choose for an enlightened policy of continuous product improvement, or cost reduction. Most of the better players do. But because these options are open to everyone, acquisition of market share has normally more to do with aggression – beating the competition into the ground by price cuts that they can't sustain, for example, or taking the (ostensibly) more gentlemanly approach of merger and acquisition. Either way, during this stage of the market two factors are evident:

- Large expenditures taking place to sustain your position;
- Concentration of market share into fewer and fewer hands.

A certain national pharmacy chain has been accused of increasing market share by opening up alongside local dispensing chemists. They are then said to destroy the profitability of the adjacent business by undercutting prices on all non-prescription business. When the unfortunate target closes down they pick up the dispensing business. Not a pleasant story and maybe not true. But it's certainly a feasible strategy.

Here again, just when everyone else is going in the direction inspired by the characteristics of this phase of the market, you should be thinking about the next phase, commodity status conditions: competition for relatively small margins based on volume availability, price and service levels. My first question would be, 'Do I want/need to be here at all?' If everyone else is intent on acquiring market share and it will soon be less and less rewarding to have that share, why not think about selling out or moving on to a new growth market now?

However, if you're determined to remain in the game you should either adjust to the idea of more intensive competition, maximize your market share now, or expect to do less and less well in this particular market (probably all three simultaneously). More intensive competition can be met by several strategies: to the basic product or service you supply you can add improvements in how you provide it, or stress how enjoyable an experience it is to buy it, and so on. There is more on this in Chapter 7.

The commodity phase

You're now in the most intensively competitive phase of the market. If you want to increase market share here (or possibly only maintain your position) you must do one of the following:

- Concentrate (acquire or merge).
- Give customers more reason to buy from you (strengthen the brand, improve customer service over the competition), in fact anything to increase what economists would call your *inelasticity of demand* – the propensity of customers to buy from *you*.
- Diversify – accept that you're not going to succeed with this product and move on to something else. This might mean extending the market as in Figure 2.3 (p. 29) or moving to something completely new.

Of course, if you've anticipated the commodity market during the earlier phases of the cycle you may have been doing all or some of this a long time ago. But now you're in the commodity phase, some of the alternative strategies that were previously open to you have been closed off.

Whichever way you look at it, conditions are qualitatively

different from what they were in earlier phases. The worst thing in the world – and what most suppliers do for far too long – is to act as if market conditions are precisely the same as they used to be. And people do that because they're not sufficiently aware of three factors:

- the strategic marketing issues we're discussing here;
- the competitive changes that have taken place around them;
- what customers want.

Refer to the example of companies A and B above. Company A was still trying to compete in the mature and commodity phases in precisely the same way as they had in the expert and growth phases – and it just didn't work.

Summary

- Markets move through their various phases through alterations in the balance of supply and demand.
- As a result of easy access to information, more and more markets are moving towards the economists' theoretical construct of the perfect market where price is the key determinant of buyer behaviour.
- If you're aware that your market is moving towards commodity status and the perfect market you will probably behave differently from how you would behave if you remain blissfully unaware. Awareness allows you to be more considered in your behaviour and to react to prospective change rather than current change.
- Adverse positions are generally capable of improvement in most, if not all, phases of the market, but the further along the curve the market moves, typically the more expensive it becomes to correct your mistakes. It's usually a better idea to plan for the outcome you want over a long period and determine your behaviour accordingly.

The general characteristics of each stage of the market, together with broad strategic options, are set out in Table 3.2.

Table 3.2   Strategies for phases of the market life cycle – a summary

	Expert	Growth	Maturity	Commodity
Typical volume supplied	Low	Growing	Growing	High
Typical margins	High	Not noticeably lower	Falling	Low
Typical numbers of suppliers	Very few	Relatively few	More	Many
Typical desired supply / demand balance	D>S	Approaching D=S	S>D	Significant desire to oversupply
Typical supplier growth aspirations	Easily satisfied	Market growing faster than supplier aspirations	Harder to achieve growth targets generically	Suppliers' aggregate growth aspirations normally far exceed market growth capacity
Typical buying criteria	Availability	Differentiated factors	Differentiated factors	Price

54

Table 3.2 continued

Common supplier behaviour	Maximize price and profit	Ignore the competition	Confusion and panic as growth aspirations go unfulfilled. Assume the good times will return	Fight aggressively for market share – price wars, promotion wars, hostile takeovers etc.
Potentially viable strategies	Maintain technological lead. Reinvest. Build brand	Continue to build brand. Maximize market share	Drive costs and price down. Consider structural issues, such as appropriateness of distribution channels. Consider acquisition of market share. Consider selling out to those seeking to increase market share	If market share is significant, remain in market competing on price, availability and service. If not, consider exit or acquisition of more market share. If not feasible, consider niche specialization to maximize market share in a part of the market

4 Some More Things you should know about Strategic Marketing

Before we go on to examine in detail the marketing and promotional tactics you may want to consider adopting, we need to deal with three other issues:

- What about all those businesses that have more than one product?
- If you are set on diversification or getting out, how do you go about selecting different things to do?
- What about entry-barred markets?

Multi-product companies and the fundamentals of strategic marketing

If you're a multi-product company the first question to address is whether your multitude of products are destined for one market or many. If you have, say, one product in each of a number of markets, the arguments in the preceding chapters broadly apply to you as stated. The difference lies in the luxury (if that's the way you view it) you have of choosing amongst your various products when it comes to making investment decisions.

But if your main business is to sell a group of products into a single market, the issues you face are likely to relate to where on the life cycle curve your various products are and how quickly they move along it. Utopia is to achieve a family of products all equally spaced out along the curve, with new products coming in at one end as old ones drop off at the other.

The Boston Matrix

There's a neat analytical tool you may like to apply to your product family (which is just as valid whether you're in one market or many); it shows how well balanced your product portfolio is. Several years ago a few clever chaps at a company called the Boston Consulting Group devised some constructive new thinking. In the way that these things work their approach has now become standard in marketing circles – almost passed into marketing folklore, you might say.

What happens, they asked, if we compare product growth prospects with product profitability? To keep things simple we'll designate two categories in each case. We'll define products as either high or low profit and as having either high or low growth prospects. The result is a matrix (4.1).

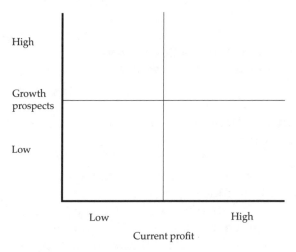

Figure 4.1   Boston Matrix categories

You can plot your products on the matrix and see what categories they fall into. 'So what?' you may ask. Consider the implications of having products in the various boxes.

In the top left-hand corner are products with plenty of potential, but they don't make much profit for you yet. These are referred to as 'problem children'. The chances are that they're going to need some investment (either in product development or market development) before they reach their potential. But in due course they'll be good news.

Once products enter the top right-hand box they're high profit and still have high growth prospects. These are characterized as 'rising stars'. You're doing well from these products now and should continue to do well in the future. This is a very good place to be (and might perhaps be reminiscent of the euphoric growth phase on the life cycle curve we talked about earlier).

Once products move into the bottom right-hand box they can still give you reasonable profits, but their days are numbered. Growth prospects by definition are not good. These products are called 'cash cows'. And on the whole the best thing to do with a cash cow is milk it for all it's worth. You effectively admit that it hasn't much further to go, so what's the point in investing heavily in it? If you choose to invest in it, this will typically be because you want to sustain its position in the market rather than improve it – so take care that your investment is likely to be repaid. However, all good things come to an end. The cash cow's profits dry up and there's nothing left to be milked. At that point you have a product with no growth prospects and little current profitability. It becomes a 'dog' (though quite why I've never understood) and there's not much point in continuing to run with it, unless with some investment it can be made to perform better (improved features, brand positioning, etc.), in which case it may well have gone full circle and it's a problem child again.

Plot your products on the matrix, and the result is Figure 4.2.

The Boston Matrix and the product life cycle
In the way we've expressed it here, a process or cycle is definitely taking place. And you may well ask why we assume that

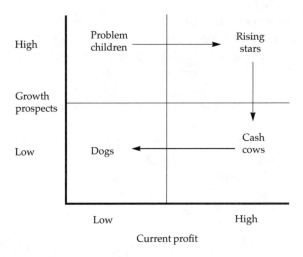

Figure 4.2   Boston Matrix cycle

products move through these various matrix categories. If we superimpose the Boston Matrix analysis on the life cycle thinking the picture is as in Figure 4.3. Again, don't forget that this is a generalization and we're talking in terms of trends and tendencies. Mathematical accuracy is probably not at issue here, but we can see the principles for what they are.

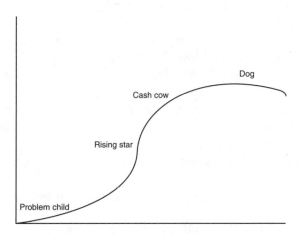

Figure 4.3   Life cycles and the Boston Matrix

The conclusion we are led to is that problem children (those difficult products that need more investment) are typically early life cycle products. Rising stars that show good profits and good growth prospects tend to congregate around the growth phase of the cycle. By the time we reach the maturity phase products are probably entering the cash cow phase and the writing's on the wall. You may be well advised to change your strategy from growing market share to milking the product (or even selling) before the poor old dog wanders into play in the commodity status market. Take care over the timing of this one in particular. You may be inclined to argue that the cash cow phase continues into the commodity market and that the dog cuts in when the market goes into decline. 'You pays your money and you takes your choice.'

How to get it wrong (but mostly people don't need any help)

Why does all this matter to the multi-product company? If you want to survive for some time to come you will be well advised to manage and balance your product portfolio carefully. On the face of it, if all your products are rising stars it may seem good news. But beware. If they all move forward together, in due course you could find yourself with a group of cash cows that may well turn into dogs in the near future.

Unfortunately, many companies don't realize the process is taking place until it's too late. When they see the dog phase coming they panic and start looking around for something new to replace the former cash cow. But finding products that come straight into the growth phase is not easy, for all the barriers-to-entry reasons considered above. Such companies are then forced to take on something new, and go through the build-up phase of the problem child before they start seeing serious return in the growth phase. It's very common indeed to come across companies with too many commodity status products at the wrong end of the curve and one or two new ones at the beginning, on which all hopes for the future are pinned. Not a comfortable place to be, particularly as it can be avoided with some thoughtful planning earlier on.

How it works in practice

Some years ago I was working with a company (company C) in the computer consumables market. The company had been started by a highly entrepreneurial salesman. If you cut the organization in half you would have seen 'sales-driven' stamped all the way through. It had done well, riding the growth curve in the computer market where the demand for consumables such as printer ribbons, disk duplication and specialist papers seemed insatiable.

The problem was that although the market was buoyant, it was hardly rocket science that company C was supplying. Ease of access kept margins to the absolute minimum and the market was undoubtedly in commodity status. Although growing, it did not offer enough generic growth potential to satisfy all suppliers' growth aspirations, and certainly not this company's growth aspirations.

Company C therefore sought to develop a new product where they had differentiation – something the competition could not offer. The chairman, who was a much travelled individual, hit upon a new PC security product in the US and quickly signed an exclusive licensing deal for his company as sole UK supplier. The management team, who knew they had problems achieving their targets through their existing range, latched enthusiastically on to the new product as the potential salvation of the company's growth aspirations. All they had to do was wait for the computer security market to take off. So they waited ... and waited. The problem was that over a two-year period the market resolutely refused to take off. Meanwhile, the commodity product range wasn't improving either.

At about this time we ran the life cycle and Boston analyses on the product range. Inevitably it emerged as in Figure 4.4.

Arguably, all products other than the new PC security product were at or approaching 'dog' category. The PC security product might have a future but would undoubtedly need a considerable amount of long-term investment to achieve the results that company C was seeking. And company C had no products that fell in the more lucrative growth and maturity phases of the market.

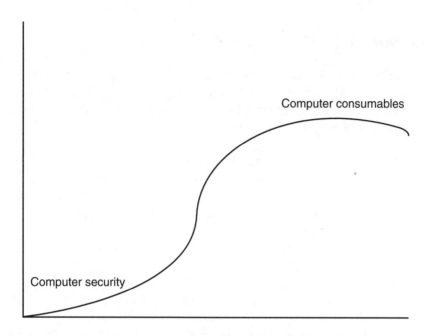

Figure 4.4   Strategic analysis of company C's product range

When we met the management team to outline our findings we presented our case and waited for comments. There was then one of those long silences during which you can't really tell if you've gained approval or not. Then everyone started speaking together and we watched scales falling from eyes.

The analysis alone offered them an effective and exciting tool for understanding the limitations that they had placed on their own performance. It also gave them the basis for finding a solution to their own problem.

I said earlier that it's usually hard to enter a market at growth or maturity – largely because that's what everyone else is trying to do, and it's this that drives the market towards commodity status. But based on this analysis company C's management was quickly able to identify a product range that they thought would do the trick (a range of disk duplication machines which were new in the national market at the time). The company's efforts were concentrated on bringing in the new range as quickly as possible, so that the business was regenerated.

Diversifying out of the market

We now consider what you should do if you've come to the conclusion that you're at the wrong stage of the life cycle to make sense of staying in the market. Bear in mind that you really have two sets of assets in your business:

1   Your 'distinctive competences' – what you have to offer that makes customers want to buy from you. That's everything that makes up your product offering, from your production facility through your unique blend of management skills to your technical know-how.
2   Your customer base – people who know and love you as a reliable supplier.

Of course, the relative importance of these assets will vary with the business that you are in. However, it's crucial that you don't undervalue either of them, particularly when you are thinking about diversification.

Suppose you've decided that the returns you're getting in your existing marketplace are not sufficient to justify your continued presence, at least in the long term. The way to diversify successfully is to study your assets and decide where they might take you. To help you do this, here's another neat piece of marketing theory, created by Professor Ansoff and known not surprisingly as the Ansoff Matrix. Like most effective theory, it seems obvious once established. The hard part is inventing it in the first place.

There are several ways of expressing the Ansoff Matrix. The approach we take here is to compare markets or customers with products or services and to categorize each as new or existing. This gives a matrix as shown in Figure 4.5. Box 1 indicates a scenario in which you're selling existing products to existing customers. It's not very exciting and the returns are not as good as you would like them to be, but at least it's familiar and therefore feels relatively safe.

But since it's not where you want to be, the question is 'How do you go about diversification?' The matrix suggests that the

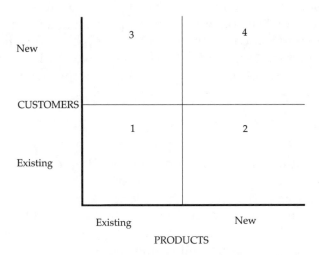

Figure 4.5   Ansoff Matrix categorization of strategic risk

safest route is either to take a box 2 strategy or a box 3 strategy. Either will offer some degree of security based on your existing asset position: either customers or products will be familiar. The bad news lies in box 4, where both markets and products are different. You have to be very keen to get out of your market to play this strategy because it's the highest-risk option available (which is not to say that it's always the wrong route to take).

The temptation is often to try to find new markets for an existing product range. But, if you have recognized that your product is in decline or shortly will be, you may merely be increasing market share in a market that is destined for death. It's all very well having 100 per cent of the 286 personal computer market, but not if no one wants to buy them any more. A better long-term strategy may be to identify new products that you can sell into your existing customer base. At least you know the customers and at least they will continue to have needs of some sort.

If you focus on this route, you have to concentrate on the customer base itself and, to my mind, this is crucial. Your customers may arguably be the most important asset you have. And when was the last time you focused on their needs and on how your organization treats them?

The strategic direction of most markets leads inexorably to the conclusion that customer service and product innovation are the most important competitive arenas for now and the early twenty-first century. And for that reason we shall give them a great deal of attention in Chapters 7 and 12 respectively.

Summary

- In a multi-product environment you should be looking for a balanced spread of products around the Boston Matrix categories and along the life cycle curve.
- If you are set on a course of diversification out of the market, look first for opportunities that capitalize on either your product expertise or your customer base.

Part II
Everything you ever Wanted to Know about Marketing but Were Afraid to Ask

My observation after looking at a lot of companies . . . is that only about 15% of their focus is on customers and not more than 5% is on competitors and the other 80% is on internal matters which only indirectly deal with customers and competitors.

William Bain, President, Bain & Co. (1984)

Map of the model

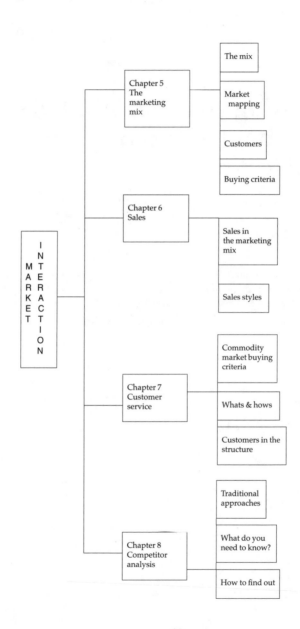

5 The Marketing Mix

We said in the Introduction that there are only three sets of factors that substantially affect how much profit you make:

1 The external environment (Part I).
2 How you communicate or interact with the market – specifically how you market and sell (the subject of Part II).
3 The efficiency and effectiveness of your production (the subject of Part III).

What is marketing?

As far as Jo Average is concerned:

marketing = advertising = waste of money.

But as you can see by now, many things in the world of profit maximization are much less cut and dried than they might initially appear.

So what is marketing if you're an important sophisticated manager?

Jo Average's view certainly needs some working on. But what about if you're at the other end of the scale? If you're a brand manager for an international conglomerate? The danger here is not that you take the naïve view but that you've got so many people, agencies and computer printouts buzzing around that you miss the wood for the trees.

Whichever end of the scale you're coming from, getting the marketing right starts with standing back just far enough to see what's going on without retreating so far that you fall off the edge of the cliff. So push the printouts to the back of the desk, put the telephone on hold and delay the meeting with the agency for a couple of hours, because we're going back to basics for a while.

What were you given as a definition of marketing at your first business seminar? Everyone has their own definition but the one I like to work with most of the time is that marketing is about getting the company to produce what people actually want to buy, in comparison with sales, which is about getting the customer to buy what you have available (no hate mail from reputable sales-people please!).

The marketing mix

At the seminar you were probably told about the 'marketing mix' – a collection of factors that you can influence or manipulate to optimize your competitive positioning in the market – in other words, your 'competitive advantages'. Back in the good old days there were said to be four elements in the marketing mix:

1   Product (or service)
2   Place
3   Promotion
4   Price (i.e. the marketplace itself).

Various people have tinkered with the list over the years but I quite like it as it is – not just because it's so alliterative that even I can remember it, but also because it emphasizes rather neatly that marketing is not merely promotion. Most of us need reminding of that fact (if we ever knew it in the first place). To optimize your profitability you need to take all the 'Ps' into account. If you're a brand manager that can be difficult. Some of these factors may well be out of your defined sphere of influence. But let's take the thinking a little further and see where it gets us.

Products and distinctive competences

You're an organization, or a division, or a brand manager operating in a competitive market. In all probability it's a commodity market and you've been here so long that you've forgotten what it's like to be on the S-curve. It's just boring flat terrain around here – the same in every direction for miles.

But as you look around the landscape you notice some other travellers going in the same direction. They look a little like you, but they're not quite the same. You have features that distinguish you from them. They're your 'distinctive competences' – the factors which make the customer buy from you rather than from the other guy. They are your differentiators. These make up the 'Product' offering in the marketing mix, not just the physical characteristics of the product itself but a whole host of other factors:

- Where I can buy it.
- What else I can buy at the same time so as to minimize my buying time.
- What volume discounts you offer.
- Whether you deliver on a Thursday.
- Whether your telephonist sounds helpful and efficient when I call.
- Whether you genuinely surprise and impress me with some aspect of what you do.

These are factors that you have perhaps never thought of as being elements in the customer's choice. If we look at them from the other end of the market – the customer's end – these are his/her 'buying criteria' – the things that make them buy one product rather than another.

It is essential to arrive at a clear understanding of what constitutes your distinctive competences, because these determine the market segments that you should be addressing. Typically people come up with phrases like 'We give a really good service' or 'We really care about the customer'. All this may be true, but there is nothing particularly distinctive about it, so it simply doesn't explain why customers buy from you. Push the thinking a little further and you may arrive at the conclusion that existing customers buy from you because they like you (that can be personal or corporate of course – it's perfectly possible to like the image of a big PLC). But this isn't enough to win new customers. Why did they buy in the first place? What has made them stick with you even when you sometimes don't quite come up to expectations?

These are the kinds of issue that are at the heart of your distinctive competences and point to how you can interact intelligently with the market to win new business. Don't make the mistake of ignoring the apparently mundane. 'I was passing the shop and saw the product' or 'I saw your ad in the Sunday paper' are common elements in the range of factors that make customers buy. How will you replicate them to generate more business?

Mapping the market

At one end of the market we have you, the producer, with your distinctive competences, and at the other we have the customer with his/her buying criteria. We can represent it as in Figure 5.1. But as we mentioned earlier, you're not the only traveller on this road. There are plenty of other suppliers out there also targeting the customers to buy from them and they have distinctive competences too – features that influence whether customers buy from them. And (horror of horrors) sometimes the customers prefer their distinctive competences to yours. And then (even worse) they buy from the other guy rather than from you. In practice therefore the market looks more as in Figure 5.2.

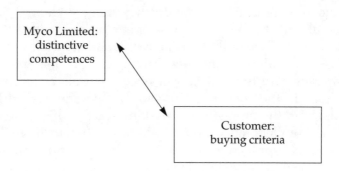

Figure 5.1   Market map – stage I

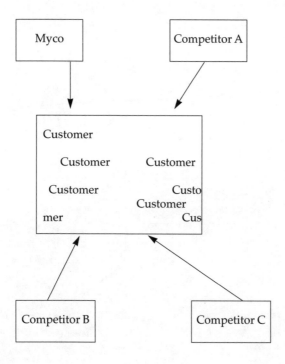

Figure 5.2   Market map – stage II

Place

If all the customers in the market have exactly the same needs and buying criteria, how do they make a choice? Surely, they would all choose the same supplier, based on the set of distinctive competences that most closely matches their needs. Clearly, they *don't* all have the same buying criteria. I shop in the supermarket with the widest aisles because I get claustrophobic. He shops in the cheapest. You shop in the one nearest home. She shops in the one with the parking spaces for mother and baby. Because customers all have slightly different buying criteria it permits suppliers to *differentiate* – or to position differently so as to appeal to those differing criteria.

Taking it one stage further we can group customers depending on their key buying criteria. We can, in effect, *segment* the market. The market map then resembles Figure 5.3. The letters represent

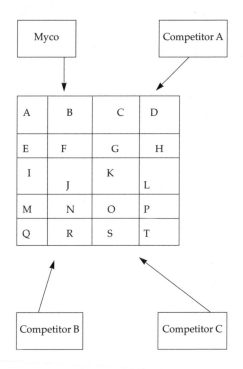

Figure 5.3   Market map – stage III

various segments of the market that you are more or less well placed to address. There are innumerable ways to segment a market. You can do it geographically, by price, by size of spend, by colour preference. In fact you can segment by anything that constitutes a buying criterion since different customers will have greater or lesser preference for particular criteria.

This segmentation process permits you to differentiate (or, as we saw in Part I, to keep the market somewhat less than perfect) or niche market. On the basis of the distinctive competences that you have or could develop, you need to identify the segments of the market that you can address most effectively and concentrate on those. The key questions here are 'What are the right segments for you?' and 'What makes you think that your distinctive competences match the buying criteria of customers in those segments?'.

Of course, if you're big and bold enough you could be addressing several segments. But you still, in general, need to address the market on a segmented basis, with products focused appropriately to each selected segment. Normally, if you try to address the market as a homogeneous unit, somebody somewhere is likely to be able to produce a more segment-specific offering than yours. And if they have a product that matches my buying criteria more closely than yours I will more than likely shift my purchasing pattern towards them. The result is that they take market share from you.

In most markets, therefore, even the largest players offer a bewildering set of variations on the basic theme. Try to buy yoghurt or industrial components and the story is the same. Segmentation and niche positioning rule the commodity market. So the kind of questions you should be asking yourself at this point are:

- How do I segment the market in a way that is meaningful for the products I produce?
- Which segments of the market am I/should I be addressing?
- What proportion of those segments buy from me?
- How would I need to change my product offering to win more of this segment or enter other segments?

- Would the cost of change be justified in the light of the gains I can reasonably expect to make?

While you're thinking about these questions you also need to bear in mind the strategic direction and position of the market and segments concerned. Consider where you want to be, not now, but in the future as well, given the performance characteristics you expect from different segments.

An example of this is the UK housing market in 1995. At the time of writing the house building sector is as flat as a pancake. It seems as if it's been this way for eternity (well, actually since about 1991, but that's an eternity for most producers of just about anything). Within the last month two PLC house building companies have announced their withdrawal from the market. It may be just a competitive ploy, but it certainly doesn't seem like it. One is simply withdrawing, the other trying to float its house building division. Obviously there's not much money to be made in this sector in 1995. But I would ask questions such as:

- Why didn't we foresee this in the 1980s and do something about it then? (Remember in Chapters 2 and 3 we discussed the difference between selling out in the maturity phase as opposed to the commodity phase?)
- Do we know enough about the way our market works to be sure that in another five years we won't look back on this decision with regret?
- How would we return to the sector later? (Unfortunately too many decisions are taken for short-term rather than the long-term reasons, which would lead to different decisions.)

Taking stock
To summarize so far: we started by saying that marketing is half the story in your interaction with the market at the point of communication. We then went on to say that marketing encompasses, but is bigger than, advertising and promotion. It consists of four main areas – product, place, price and promotion.

We discussed the product angle and related it to the place question. We said that the best strategy is to marry the differentiators that make up your product with the segments of the market that select by those factors – equating your distinctive competences to the buying criteria of customers in various market segments.

A bit more about 'places' – customers and markets

At this point someone somewhere will be screaming out 'But how do I know why customers buy?'. The answer is that you ask them . . . and sometimes you even believe them. But you do more than just believe them. You also observe them – now and over time – and you come to understand them. As far as asking them is concerned, it is now fashionable to conduct surveys and tele-phone interviews. Large organizations are becoming increas-ingly aware of what small companies have always known – that they live or die by giving customers what they want. And that's no bad thing. Much of the information we, as consultants, feed back to clients is gleaned from customer surveys.

Some time ago we undertook a survey (mostly by telephone) for a large firm of architects. I always make sure that I carry out at least a proportion of these customer contacts personally, and on this occasion my list included an employee in the estates depart-ment of an extremely well-known UK insurance company. The person was reluctant to disclose his real opinions until I made it clear that we were working on behalf of the firm and were not part of it. He checked with me that his responses would not be directly attributed to him and then started to tell the truth. The rest of the conversation began with 'Working with them has been a nightmare' and continued in much the same vein for several minutes.

Unfortunately it wasn't just this customer that felt this way. After several more calls of a broadly similar nature we were in a position to feed back the awful truth to the client. They weren't too pleased but the information was vital to the repositioning of the business and they certainly wouldn't have had direct access to it themselves.

While we're on the subject, what is your organization's atti-tude towards complaints? Do you view them as negative? An irritant? Or do you see them as valuable feedback? If you set a customer service standard of reducing the number of complaints, everyone in the organization learns that complaints are a bad thing and you lose feedback. Complaints are even suppressed. How much better to focus on the causes of complaints and correct those!

You may also be surprised (if not a little miffed) by the results you get when you start talking to customers. Some time ago we undertook customer research for a highly respected design agency. Before we started they were firmly of the view that customers bought from them because they were superior designers. What customers actually said, when asked, was that design was taken for granted in deciding where to place their business. The assumption was that designers wouldn't be in the market if they weren't competent and the buyers had more than enough experience to know. The key buying criterion was speed of response. Customers needed to drop off a brief by 9.00 a.m. and receive the design by the end of the working day – or more commonly fax the brief through at 4.00 p.m. on a Friday (often with very little warning) and receive the results by 8.00 a.m. on Monday.

When you're a professional it's rather a blow to the pride to be told that customers buy for some reason other than your professional skill – but it's certainly better to know than not to know, because you can then address the key buying criteria that really do determine purchase decisions.

Promotion

We now come to that thorniest of issues – promotion, or advertising – the persuasive bit. People think that if they get this bit right everything else will be right. I hope that by this stage you'll be aware that promotion is pointless without the right product for the market segments you're addressing. If you are failing to address the customer's buying criteria, no amount of promotion will make up for it.

A company I once knew used to over-promise and under-deliver consistently, i.e. they would regularly promise customers more than they could deliver. Their sales and promotional skills were good, so they regularly won new customers. The problem was that very few customers stayed with them for more than three months. That was long enough to find out that the organization could not deliver what it promised.

The moral of the story is to perfect your product offering and target the appropriate segments of the market *before* you think about promoting what you do. Then you can turn to the question of promotion with confidence. Table 5.1 lists typical promotional tools. Each of these can be broken down still further depending on the market you're in. The single most important issue in the context of using promotional tools is to use those that are most appropriate to the market segment you are addressing. What constitutes the right tools will vary from segment to segment and for a given segment over time.

Table 5.1 Typical promotional tools

Brochure	– corporate – product	**Events**	– exhibitions – conferences – seminars
Public relations			
		Newsletters	
Advertising	– press – radio – TV – electronic	**Video**	
		Referral	
Direct mail		**Sales force**	
Telemarketing & telesales		**Sponsorship**	

During the buoyant 1980s most successful businesses were targeting turnover increases, often with little thought of the costs of doing so. In the pursuit of turnover, marketing budgets were commonly increased to figures that now look astronomic. The modern trend is for organizations to look much more critically at marketing expenditure. At one level this means placing your promotional budget with the organization that delivers most for the price. At another level it means completely rethinking how you promote your product. Information technology has its impact here too, allowing you to target finer and finer groups of customers according to finer and finer sets of buying criteria.

The observable result of this attention to detail is that promotional spending is less frequently being wasted on blunt tools such as mass advertising and increasingly invested in more incisive methods such as telemarketing and direct mail. Not only are the latter more focused; they are also easier to measure. If you run a big advertising campaign and customer spending rises how sure can you be that the two factors are as linked as you'd wish? If you run a direct mail campaign you can measure the number of freepost returns.

Given present technology and selling environments, there are many products that do not readily lend themselves to such focused promotion. But as microtechnology marches on I find myself asking how long this will continue to be the case. Whatever the effect of technology, the same question will always apply: 'Which promotional tools are most appropriate for my product in my marketplace?' Information technology will only ever alter the answer – not the need to ask it. And the answer will lie in the customer's buying criteria and buying methodology. Even if the customers themselves don't know what their buying criteria are, they still use them. There is still a reason why they choose product A rather than product B.

Typical of the kinds of question you need to ask here are the following. Ask yourself in each case what an appropriate promotional strategy would be to address the buying criteria for each one.

1   *Impulse or planned purchase?* Consider the buying criteria that apply to buying ice cream on a hot day as compared to selecting a central heating system. Ask:

   ● *Which buying criteria?*
   ● *Which promotional strategy?*

2   *Want or need?* Take care over this one. I may need a given product – say car insurance – but the necessity applies to the generic product category, not my choice of supplier or product. Ask:

- *Which buying criteria?*
- *Which promotional strategy?*

3 *Large budget item or small?* Typically a much longer decision chain applies to the purchase of a major computer system than repeat purchase of stationery. There are also likely to be more decision-takers with a greater variety of buying criteria in a large-budget purchase. Ask:

- *Which buying criteria?*
- *Which promotional strategy?*

4 *Informed or uninformed purchaser?* If I am an inexperienced purchaser I shall tend to rely on advice. That may in some cases be independent advice, but more often I shall seek advice from the supplier (or perhaps several). Consider a retail purchase of a consumer durable. Buying a freezer is not something I do every week, so I tend to rely for advice on the retailer. I have two nearly simultaneous decisions to take: which product and which retailer? Often, the retailer that positions more effectively as an expert will get my business because of the sense of trust and reliance I am building up. In a case such as this I may well have buying criteria I was not aware of. Ask:

- *Which buying criteria?*
- *Which promotional strategy?*

5 *Single purchaser or group decision?* Is this my choice alone or am I making the decision in concert with others? In this context you must ascertain the nature of the decision-making process. Maybe you have to make a series of sequential purchase decisions. Person A decides whether you appear on the tender list. Group B decides whether you get on the short list. But the board makes the decision from among the final three. In each case there are buying criteria and each decision is susceptible to some form of promotion. I have often found that the successful supplier is the one with enough stamina to continue to

treat the process as a marketing issue through the purchase decision period. Ask:

- *Which buying criteria?*
- *Which promotional strategy?*

6   *Repeat purchase or one-off?* This relates to the question of purchaser experience. If it's a one-off, I am likely to be an inexperienced purchaser. I may well place considerable emphasis on the perceived reliability of the supplier (how well you've established your corporate identity). If the purchase is one I make weekly I shall build up expertise in the buying process. I shall usually establish some kind of relationship with the supplier – real or imagined – which amounts to inertia. Once the inertia is established it takes something specific to drive me to another supplier. Think about company A in Chapter 3. Its customers' buying criteria included inertia resulting from the cost of supplier substitution. When the cost of substitution became less significant, other criteria – particularly price – came into play.

At the time of writing it's fashionable to criticize the high street banks for the way they have treated small business customers during the recession of the early 1990s. But an interesting fact is that most banking customers don't change banks by choice. Banking is an inertia purchase. Once I have established my relationship it's complex to change and I am unlikely to do so without good reason. As it happens, I did change banks – after 18 years as an established customer. But I'll save that story for Chapter 7 on customer service. Ask:

- *Which buying criteria?*
- *Which promotional strategy?*

7   *Long decision frame or instantaneous?* From a supplier's point of view, it can be infuriating when customers take a long time to reach a decision. But some products are just like that. Often it's price related. If my purchase represents a significant spend, a complex set of buying criteria will be involved and

nothing will force me to a quick decision. Equally, the customer's decision to purchase or not may depend on some factor beyond his control. And if it's beyond his control, the chances are that it's beyond yours as well. In these circumstances your promotional strategy is probably best focused on achieving preferred supplier status – so that if the uncontrollable event does occur you are selected for the contingent purchase. Ask:

- *Which buying criteria?*
- *Which promotional strategy?*

This list of questions is by no means exhaustive. Extend it as appropriate to your own market segment and determine the mix of promotional tools, programmes and so on that are most appropriate for you now. Repeat the procedure periodically, because assuredly the optimal promotional mix will change over time. The more you can do to establish in your own and the company's mind that customer needs and preferences change, the more likely you are to survive and prosper. Refer to what we said about building in change in Chapter 1. Surely the principle applies here more than anywhere.

Price

Back in Chapter 3 we looked at the way that economists view price. We concluded that in any given market real price (i.e. adjusted for inflation) will tend to be competed down over the life cycle curve towards a level which gives suppliers a 'normal profit' – the minimum level they will accept and still stay in the market.

We also concluded that this happens when suppliers don't have 'market power', i.e. so long as there are no *imperfections* in the market that keep price artificially high. This leads suppliers to try to create imperfections – brand loyalty and so on – with the aim of making customers prefer their products over otherwise similar products available from other suppliers.

Finally, we concluded that most markets are coming closer and closer to commodity status – the economists' theoretical perfect market in which differentiation is substantially impossible. I tend to think of the perfect market as resembling absolute zero – you can get closer and closer to it but you never actually reach it.

So where does all this leave you as far as your pricing strategy is concerned? I should remind you at this point that the purpose of this book is not to reinvent the wheel: the theoretical basis of pricing is well established and there are plenty of good books on pricing theory and strategy. What we need to do here instead is to think about how pricing affects your profit level.

It will come as no surprise to find that the most profitable pricing strategy will depend on the position of your market on the life cycle curve and the particular performance characteristics exhibited by the market segments you address.

Price is discretionary

The first point to make is, on the face of it, obvious: price is a variable in the marketing mix. This implies that it is discretionary. You as supplier can choose the price you set (unless you operate in a price-controlled market – but these are now a rarity in the free market economy). Of course, I as customer also have a choice – whether to buy at the price you want to charge or take my business elsewhere. Nevertheless, too many suppliers seem to forget that they must make a decision on price and that the decision is not automatic. The usual knee-jerk reaction is that if your supply prices rise, they must be passed on. Or, in a very competitive market, if you don't match the price the other guy is charging, you'll sell nothing. Often of course, these points describe the practical reality of the situation – but not always.

An issue, but not the only one

The main thing to realize is that you do have a choice. Therefore you need to make the decision thoughtfully. The presupposition that you have no choice assumes that purchase decisions are always price-determined. I would argue, however, that although price is always one element in the mix of buying criteria it is rarely the only element. People *say* that price is the most important factor but often *behave* as though it is not. Think about the last time you spent a sum of money that was significant to you, either personally or corporately. Was price part of the decision? Probably yes. But was it the only element in the decision? For most people the answer is 'no'. If you had been a supplier of that item, what could you have done to influence the non-price elements in the buying decision? It doesn't take long to think of something else in the marketing mix that makes you attractive as a supplier without having to jerk the knee and reduce price. Now, go through exactly the same process for something you have purchased recently that is not a significant item to you. If anything, the decision in this case is even less price-driven.

No doubt you know someone (perhaps you are that someone!) to whom price is the overriding determinant of buying behaviour. Recognize that such a customer is simply at one end of the range of buying criteria. It may help to think of it like this: take any pair of possible buying criteria, say price and proximity to

Price ——————————————— Proximity

Figure 5.4   Mapping buying criteria

home, and map them as in Figure 5.4. Any customer in the market will fall somewhere along this continuum – more motivated by price, less by proximity or vice versa. Undoubtedly some will position themselves at the extreme ends: those that will cross the world to buy the cheapest and those that won't even cross the road to get a low price. You could argue that everyone has a slightly different combination of preferences. But for practical purposes we can categorize by dividing the line into segments and grouping customers into those that are more or less motivated by price against proximity. This is how to segment markets.

Similarly, we could map another set of buying criteria at right angles to the configuration in Figure 5.4 and produce a matrix – choose the criteria yourself and think about the combinations it yields. You might be able to generate axes for any buying criteria you chose and produce a multidimensional map on which you could plot your perfect positioning. There are mind-boggling possibilities for the computer buff with more time than he knows what to do with. But then you have to come down to earth and get on with the practical job of setting your prices!

Setting price in practice

How, then, do you decide what price to charge? By all means learn about the theoretical background to pricing by reading one of the numerous books on the subject. Recognize, however, that customers are usually interested not so much in an absolute price for an item as in whether it falls within an acceptable price range. Someone in the competitive market sets the benchmark price for the industry. Commonly it's the lowest price offered by a supplier. From there, all manner of price/non-price combinations in the marketing mix will be applicable in different segments of the market. You should therefore:

- establish a clear idea of your target segments and their preferences and characteristics;
- Offer the price that fits those target segments most closely whilst meeting your own gross profit needs; and
- use a promotional mix that is most appropriate to the communication style and the decision-making style of the segment.

And finally . . .

Of course, there are markets and segments where differentiation is in practice very difficult. Some time ago I wanted to buy a particular brand of TV set. I visited London's Tottenham Court Road where every other shop sold TVs. Nearly all such shops offered the set I wanted at prices within 3–4 per cent of one another. But there was one shop that sold nothing but my chosen manufacturer's products. Out of interest I dropped in, only to find that the set was priced at the manufacturer's recommended list price – some 20 per cent above the discount price available all along the road. 'Why', I enquired innocently, 'ought I to buy from you when I could buy more cheaply next door?' I was expecting to hear about some kind of special guarantee or support scheme, favoured customer status or whatever. After a moment's hesitation a look of weariness came over the sales assistant's eyes, as if he'd had this conversation numerous times before. 'Well, sir,' came the answer, 'you must buy wherever you feel most comfortable.' I enquired further as to what factors I ought to consider in deciding where I would be most comfortable but no reply was forthcoming. In effect, the shop was trading on manufacturer's brand name alone. And yet all the benefits of the same brand name were available next door for 20 per cent less. Being more than a little price-sensitive, I bought my set in one of the other shops. The retailer in question has now gone out of business.

Summary

- The best place to start analysing how well you interact with your market is still the traditional marketing mix of product, place, promotion and price.
- Your product consists not just of the physical item itself but the full range of characteristics that make up your 'distinctive competences' – your total offering to the customer. How clear are you about what constitutes your product offering and why customers buy it?
- When you have identified those segments of the market to which your product is most appropriate, you may have to change some characteristics of your offering to match what the targeted market segments are looking for.
- Customers will buy according to their own buying criteria and will select from the suppliers on offer based on those criteria. How successful you are will depend fundamentally on how well you match your offering to the buying criteria of key customer groups.
- All the thinking here needs to be put in the context of the market life cycle. Different market segments may well be moving through the life cycle at different rates, making them more or less attractive to you.
- Finding out why customers buy is a critical part of your decision-making process. When was the last time you tried to

establish your customers' buying criteria? Frequently they differ from what you as supplier might think.

- Promotion is usually seen as the first and most important element in the marketing mix. Unless your product offering and marketplace are correctly matched, you're wasting your time and your promotional budget.

- However, when you have reached the point of planning promotion, select those tools and channels of communication that best address the decision-making process of your target segments. These will vary enormously depending on the nature of the purchase.

- In most commodity markets price is commonly taken as a given factor – it's assumed that there's nothing you can do about it. Consequently suppliers often approach the subject unintelligently. It is far better to see price for what it is – one of a number of elements in the marketing mix (the supplier's viewpoint) and the buying decision (the customer's viewpoint). Looked at in this way, price becomes more of a variable to be manipulated interdependently than simply an unpleasant fact of life.

- When establishing the buying criteria of your targeted segments, mapping price against other variables will provide a pointer to the significance of price in the purchase decision.

6 Sales in the Marketing Mix

I shall now make a statement that is virtually guaranteed to generate large volumes of hate mail from the sales profession:

> Sales is no more and no less than a communication tool, one of a number of tools that you use to interact with your market. Successful sales activity depends on the extent to which you understand this premise.

Probably the single most significant error I have encountered in business is the belief that the solution to all problems lies in selling more – if only we could shift more volume of product everything would be all right.

In pursuit of sales volume, people tend to do very strange things. They underprice. They over-promise. They do a lot of unpleasant and unmentionable things which would be unnecessary if they had used the right ingredients in the recipe right from the start:

● an understanding of the structure of the market and how it is moving so as to position themselves appropriately;

- the communication mix;
- the control of production.

Sales activity is seen as a panacea. It is not. When used inappropriately it's like an untrained violinist playing loudly in a symphony orchestra: so preoccupied with his/her role, to the exclusion of all others, that he/she destroys the effect of the whole. It's too late to get my money back for this performance, but I won't come to hear this orchestra again, no matter how good the rest of the members are.

Having said this, when used in the right way in the right context, sales activity can provide the climax of the symphony. Let me emphasize again that the purpose of this book is not to tell you how to be a better sales person. Libraries have been filled on that subject already. Rather, let's use the time here to consider how sales activity can be harmoniously and effectively integrated into the orchestra of profitable business management.

Balancing the harmonies

My general observation of the sales function across businesses of various kinds is that it tends, more than any other part of the business machine, to be out of balance. Usually it's either playing too loudly or it can't be heard at all.

Why should this be? Perhaps it's because sales is the most overt interface between the business and the outside world. Accordingly, it's the part of the business that is most likely to highlight any misalignment between what you are providing and what the market is asking for. If you're misaligned but asking the sales department to sell, you're placing a tall order on it. You will be complaining at it for underperformance and the customers will feed their dissatisfaction back to you through the sales department – if you're ready to listen, that is. By contrast, if the business is producing what the customer wants to buy sales can provide you with the sweetest harmonies of all.

Typically, the business in which the sales department is playing too loudly are those that have been founded upon a sales culture, often by entrepreneurial salespeople. In these circumstances (for example, commonly in the office equipment market) all the focus is on sales turnover. Management reports (if any) emphasize turnover to the virtual exclusion of all other activities of the business. In this kind of environment it's almost certain that something else somewhere else in the company will go wrong (often customer service and/or financial control) and no one will notice. The business will sink slowly under the waves with the first violin still playing valiantly.

The other extreme (common in professional business – solicitors, architects, accountants and so on) is that sales is just not on the agenda. To mention sales is somehow improper or unprofessional. The tradition is that you wait to be asked before offering. You speak when you're spoken to and not before. Admittedly, much of this has started to change over the last few years as professional marketplaces have become increasingly competitive. But my observation is that the improvement is driven far more by necessity than desire and that there is still a long way to go in most professional businesses.

Given these two extremes, we might consider drawing a matrix of sales styles, comparing a business's degree of customer orientation with its level of proactivity in sales (see Figure 6.1). Depending on whether your business has a customer service

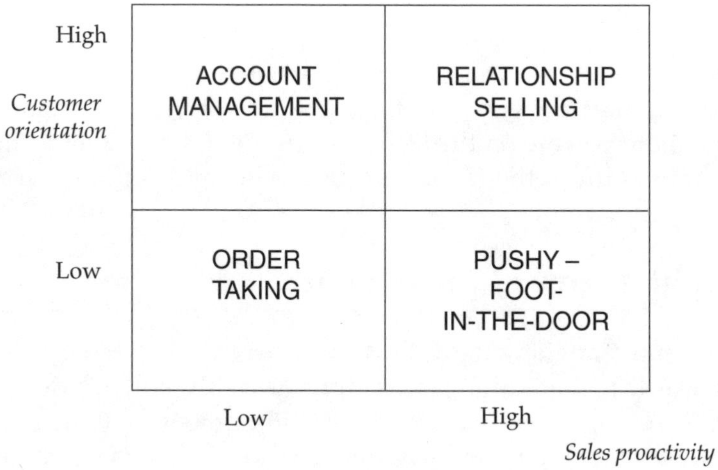

	Low	High
High *Customer orientation*	ACCOUNT MANAGEMENT	RELATIONSHIP SELLING
Low	ORDER TAKING	PUSHY – FOOT-IN-THE-DOOR

Sales proactivity

Figure 6.1　Sales styles

orientation or not and depending on how proactive it is in sales terms, you can position your sales style. Do you do no more than sit and take orders? Are you the 'foot-in-the-door' type of organization that will rarely make a follow-up sale? Maybe you take customer issues more seriously and adopt an account management style. Or perhaps you see yourselves as relationship salespeople.

The questions to ask here are:

- What are you trying to achieve through the sales function – and is your current sales strategy giving it to you?

- What stage of the life cycle are you at and what sales strategy is most appropriate, given your short- and long-term objectives?

Only you, the management, can determine the route you want your business to take. It seems to me that achieving what you need from sales activity starts with proportioning it correctly in comparison with the other parts of the business. Therefore, before we go any further, ask yourself this simple question:

- Is the sales function given the right degree of prominence in our business?

Only you can answer that, since what constitutes 'right' varies from market to market (and – you've guessed it – since it depends on where you are on the life cycle curve). If the answer is 'no', it's time to examine the whole question of how you approach selling.

The right degree of prominence

To some readers, what follows will seem unbelievably straightforward. If that's the case, you're probably either from a sales background or you work in an environment in which sales is emphasized. If so, the main question to address is whether sales is *over*-emphasized in your organization. Remember that the process of business is systemic. Optimal performance will come when the whole organism is in balance internally and in the market environment. Then each part reacts sympathetically with every other and no one element is over-prominent so as to tip the balance and leave the organization weakened and performing less effectively.

Strange though it may seem in a competition-driven universe, many organizations still find it difficult to appreciate the need to sell. So let's look at some of the factors that you should consider if you are to establish a successful sales policy and function in the context of planned, coordinated marketing activity.

The 'right degree of prominence' is something that has to be established on a case-by-case basis. How do you do it? Start by asking yourself how business is generated in your organization. In many instances the answer will be, 'Well, business has traditionally just come in'. But more often than not that will be followed by, 'But it doesn't seem to be doing so to the same degree that it used to'. Now, think about the ground we covered in Part I about the balance of supply and demand in the context of market life cycles. If you're in a market that has been passing through a growth phase for some time it may not be particularly surprising that business has arrived of its own accord. Similarly, if you're in an occupation that in some sense has benefited from barriers to entry (say solicitors or accountants) the ratio of supply to demand has been kept artificially low.

Under such circumstances sales, which is regarded as a rather unpleasant business anyway, is usually relegated to the area of 'I Don't Have To Think About This Now'. But when the environment changes you need the flexibility to modify your approach to the way you do business. And in many cases that will start with the need to increase the weight you give to the whole issue of business generation – and not least sales.

Thus addressing this issue of the right degree of prominence often first requires an emotional adjustment. We must sell to survive.

The buck stops ... somewhere

When that emotional adjustment has been made, ask yourself this next question: 'Who is responsible for achieving sales in our organization?'

In organizations in which sales is a problem, this question is usually answered in one of two ways: either 'the other guy – because I'm really not suited to it' or 'we all are'. Both answers are satisfactory so long as certain conditions are met. However, usually I get worried at this point because those conditions are often absent. First, if it really is 'the other guy' and not you, are you sure he's aware of it? How do you know he is? If he's sitting there thinking exactly the same about you, then there is no responsibility for sales. Second, if we're all responsible for sales, specifically in what way is each of us responsible? Candidates will be failed for answering 'in as many ways as possible' to this question!

Both questions need specific answers if your organization is to survive and prosper in the commodity market in which most of us operate. And it is vital to link sales activity to personal performance. The organization's sales budget must be capable of being broken down progressively to a point where someone somewhere is responsible for the achievement of all parts in it. (No budget? Go to Chapter 10 before reading further.)

In organizations not used to having to sell, the idea of personal responsibility for sales is most difficult to swallow. It's not uncommon for such organizations to take the view that the allocation of personal responsibility would be divisive, maybe even terminally so. This has never been the case in my experience. In any event, personal responsibility can exist within group accountability. It seems to me that failing to achieve the level of sales the organization needs to survive is far more dangerous than failing to make cultural readjustments to the need for more clearly defined individual responsibility.

The best person for the job is ...

Let's assume that we've bitten the bullet and accepted the concept of personal sales targets. From concept to implementation can be a significant leap. You may take the view that no one in the organization (especially you) is ideally suited to selling. But if that's the case you are tacitly admitting that the organization is no longer appropriately structured for the market environment in which it finds itself. And if that's the case some structural change is obviously in order. The structural change will imply bringing new people on board or retraining those already there. And, particularly if you're a professional organization, you should think in terms of starting at the top.

The final issue

If you've read this far without tearing up the book in disgust there's one final issue to address – sales motivation. Traditional organizational cultures often have difficulty in understanding the concept of staff motivation.

Business owners and senior managers normally have enough motivation – their necks are on the line and that tends to concentrate the mind. In more recent years the same has applied to staff as well, due to the threat of redundancy. But it seems to me that as an economy we've lost something by changing from carrot to stick. People never perform as well from a base of fear as they do from a root of desire. Therefore more emphasis should be put on motivation.

It's for you (and your sales staff) to determine the rewards for excellent performance. Make sure that the reward is sufficient to guarantee the level of performance you need.

Summary

- The objective you should be seeking if you want to optimize profits is the achievement of harmonious balance, both among the various functions of your organization and between the organization and the outside world.

- To maintain that harmony requires flexibility. Flexibility will enable you to respond to external change by altering the balance among the various internal factors in the organization so as to maintain the optimal relationship with the outside world. Without this flexibility you will lose profit.
- The sales function is often out of balance, either overemphasized or underemphasized, depending on the dominant culture within the organization.
- If your organization overemphasizes the sales function, balance it by increasing emphasis on the other elements discussed in this book.
- If you are part of a culture that has traditionally underemphasized sales, first be sure that you genuinely adopt the view that the business needs to increase that emphasis.
- Go on to consider where sales responsibility lies within the business. All the sales budget should be capable of being laid at someone's door.
- Be clear that those individuals and teams who are responsible for sales are adequately equipped for their role in the business. This is essentially a matter of training and motivation.
- Make sure that your structure, training, motivation and monitoring deliver your objective of profit maximization.

7 Customer Service

Taking Stock

Let's break off from the main thread of the argument for a moment and take stock. We started (in the introduction) by advancing the proposition that there are three categories of factors that influence the amount of profit you make. We said that profitability depends fundamentally on how you relate to each of these key elements.

The first, the subject of Part I, was the external or strategic environment in which you function. We noted that most organizations are unable to influence significantly the major forces that are at play here. The crucial point is to understand the causes and nature of the changes and flows that are taking place and to respond sympathetically to them. In general, if you act in harmony with these macro forces, you stand a better chance of succeeding than if you attempt to swim against the tide.

In Part II we have moved on to consider your interaction with the external environment – issues concerning marketing and communication. This is something you *can* influence, because you have control (though many organizations seem unaware of this) of the communication messages you are sending out into the market. In this context we said in Chapter 5 that you need to orchestrate the key elements in your marketing mix to ensure you play the melodies that you want the market to hear. Chapter 6 then proceeded to survey – deliberately briefly – the part that sales activity needs to play in that context.

There are two other elements that we must now deal with to complete our tour of your interaction with the market: competitor analysis (since you interact with the market in competition with others), the subject of Chapter 8, and customer service, the subject here.

The commodity market, customer choice and customer service

If you're part of a very go-ahead company you may think some of what follows is 'old hat'. I want to discuss these issues here specifically because I think that you're still in the minority. Quite simply, most companies we come across either in business or coincidentally have little or no understanding of customer service. Thus, even if the ideas here are familiar, let's revisit them in the knowledge that they still form a crucial element in the competitive matrix that you should be using in the commodity market.

We mentioned in Chapter 2 that in the commodity market in which most of us operate there are primarily three factors over which you can compete (the buying criteria):

- Price
- Availability
- Service.

Remember our definition of the commodity market: a market in which, left to themselves, customers will perceive no appreciable difference between the product offerings of competing suppliers. Take as an example the video recorder market (but bear in mind that the analysis applies equally well to business-to-business activities). If I want to buy a new video recorder I can walk into any one of maybe ten high street or out-of-town outlets and choose amongst perhaps a dozen brands. Each offers much the same product. How, therefore, do I establish my buying criteria?

Maybe the first issue I will address is price. I may well have a limited budget for the purchase, so I consider all the machines that fall within the relevant range. I then notice that all the main manufacturers have a product within that price range. In fact, what distinguishes the price bands is the complexity of features implicit in the product. But the main manufacturers have segmented the market and have developed a product for each segment. I am still left with the choice.

Once price is no longer the basis for differentiation, I shall probably select on some aspect of service – the non-core features of the product. These can range from the length of guarantee to the corporate image of the supplier to the helpfulness of the receptionist last time I telephoned for product information. But very often the elements that matter most are those to do with the way in which I am handled as a customer in the shop.

Whatever the final arbiter of choice, the key distinction here is between core and non-core features of the supply package. You can only compete to a certain extent on product features and price. After that non-core features take centre-stage.

Non-core competition – the 'whats' and 'hows' of the purchase decision

When we run training seminars on customer service it's often interesting to note the different perceptions people have of why customers buy their products as compared to why they themselves buy other people's.

Commonly, people perceive their customers buy for core 'physical' reasons – the features of the product – what it is, what it does, the performance spec, whether you can get it in green or on a Thursday. Ask them about their own reasons for buying and you frequently get a different story. While the physical features play a key part in the buying decision, non-core 'service' issues are normally a significant element in the purchase choice: how easy it is to deal with the organization; how helpful they are; whether they appear interested in you as an individual customer; whether they appear polite and helpful. These are relationship aspects of the transaction.

If you ask these questions for long enough a pattern begins to emerge. Customers certainly do buy the physical features of the product. But more and more these are taken for granted. They expect the product to work, to do the job it was designed to do. They expect it to be in stock. They expect it to be available for market price. These are the 'whats' of the purchase decision. However, other influences are also at work in the decision to buy, whether the buyer is aware of them or not. These influences concern *how* the transaction is undertaken by the supplier. They are the 'hows' of the purchase decision, or the service features, and they are at least as important to the selection of the supplier as the 'whats' or physical features.

As I look around the marketplaces of the developed world it seems to me that some markets and some suppliers have caught on much more readily to the need to address the service aspects of purchase decisions than others. Some suppliers are a joy to transact business with and others are a nightmare. Most seem to understand the need to perfect the core features of the product. But many have yet to realize that their future is also made or broken on the basis of the degree of service – or attitude – the 'hows' that are embodied in my interaction with their organization. And in a commodity market where the ability to differentiate seems to diminish day by day, this factor is crucial.

All this is not to say that competition on core features of your product is unimportant. Far from it. I believe that those organizations that do not innovate will die and it's essential to keep at the leading edge of your industry's technology. Chapter 12 deals with this in more detail. But the issue here is that physical competition no longer yields the competitive advantage that it once did. And that in turn implies that you need to look for new opportunities to differentiate.

As I indicated at the end of Part I, my suspicion is that within the foreseeable future there will be only two main areas for differentiation and the creation of competitive advantage: excellence of service, and the ability to learn and develop – and thereby innovate.

Balancing service and physical issues

I said earlier that the correctness of the physical features of your product are often taken for granted. Unless they are perfect, you won't even reach first base because a buyer simply starts with the assumption that everyone gets that much right. I am never surprised to find clean cutlery when I sit down in a restaurant – it's simply something I expect – a physical feature of the 'product' the restaurant is providing.

Let me also make it clear at this stage that this distinction between physical and service issues applies as much to service industries as it does to product suppliers. I expect my insurance to work in much the same way as I expect my car to work. I also expect my restaurant meal to be cooked properly. These are the 'physical' features of the service industry. But equally there is a service aspect to the way in which service products are provided. The insurance clerk can make me feel good about buying from his company; the waiter can be offhand with me. Both influence the perception of service as readily as if I were buying physical products.

So, think of the service element as the differentiator. If everyone else is perfecting the physical aspects, only the service aspect is left as an opportunity for developing distinct competitive advantage. And some companies make an art form of perfecting the service.

The most interesting feature to note here, though, is the effect that various combinations of the physical and service aspects have on customer satisfaction:

- If I get the physical and the service features right the customer's clearly happy – and hopefully comes back.
- If I fail on both counts (say the product doesn't work and my staff have been rude), it's extremely bad news and I deserve to lose the customer.

- If I succeed on the physical features but fail on the service features (e.g. working product, uninterested staff), the customer
  can still go away with a bad taste in the mouth and may not
  come back next time, preferring to do business with someone
  more helpful, despite my excellent product.

Interestingly, though, it's sometimes the case that if I fail on the
physical features (say the product is faulty) but I recover well
when the customer complains and succeed on the service features (say I show a genuinely caring attitude and deliver the
replacement faster than promised), the final result can be a
strengthening of the relationship. See the section on dealing with
individuals at the end of this chapter (p. 106) for more details.

However, if you want to be in the lead on this aspect, you must
focus on 'right first time' – so that recovery doesn't become an
issue in the first place.

Just how bad can it get?

If it's true that the way in which you deal with people fundamentally influences their purchase decisions, it follows that anything
that you can do to improve the purchase experience for the
customer is likely to improve the sales performance of your
organization.

In dealing with this issue, let me tell a personal story about
service quality – though I think it's one many people could tell
with very few variations. From the age of 17, I had been a customer of a certain high street bank. The banks had wooed me
because they know that most of us are relatively reluctant to
change banks once our financial affairs are settled. In those days
the selection of a bank was normally a lifetime decision: it's very
inconvenient to change all the standing orders, direct debits, card
numbers and all the paraphernalia that are required for modern
financial transactions.

I remained a customer of the bank for many years and had no
reason to change. Occasionally I would make a mistake and they
behaved reasonably. Occasionally they would make a mistake

and I would be understanding. When they recovered well – and I was taken out to lunch more than once – the relationship strengthened. Over the years I was broadly satisfied and they (quite rightly) made a good profit on my accounts.

But then the recession of the early 1990s took hold. The transformation that came over the banks was like the emergence of a werewolf at full moon. It wasn't that my business had problems. Far from it. Consultancies perform at least as well in times of recession as they do in periods of growth. The problem was that so many other people's businesses were doing badly. Now nobody minds vigilance, but vigilance rapidly metamorphosed into offhandedness and offhandedness soon became downright rudeness.

The problem for the bank, as far as our business was concerned, was that we ran a number of accounts and we ran them in rather different ways. Business accounts were always in credit – often substantially. We never gave personal accounts the same degree of attention and they sometimes slipped over their limits. But the bank's technology never seemed to permit its staff to appreciate that in aggregate *they* owed *us* money. All they seemed to be aware of was that an account had gone over the limit.

Being rather easy-going, we tolerated the curt letters for some time. But there's always a last straw and they finally sent it to us. At that point we demanded an apology for a quite outrageously worded communication. . .and failed to procure it. Only when we threatened to take that matter up with a full board director was any attention paid to us, and then the letter was worded so as to justify rather than apologize for the action, in case we carried out our threat. At no time did there seem to be any interest in retaining the accounts (and we estimated our lifetime value to the bank from that point forward at over £20,000) let alone providing a quality service. So we declined to do further business with them and moved all our accounts to a new supplier.

The title of this section is 'Just how bad can it get?'. I'm sure that you'll have had even worse experiences and I'd be very interested to hear them.

So how do we do it better?

Of course, those that are often on the receiving end of this type of criticism may feel they're being unfairly castigated for infrequent and minor underperformances. However, the point to note here is that corporate reputations are more often made by bad news stories than good. My bank might have a thousand satisfied customers against me as the only disgruntled one, but the folklore of reputation will still ensure that it's the bad news that gets out. It is said that we tell three people on average about good service, but eleven about bad service. Extrapolate that geometrically through the market and it becomes easy to understand why bad news travels fast.

Doing it better starts with attitude

This refers to both the personal and the organizational level. An organization's structure often looks as in Figure 7.1. Organizational culture – that's 'attitudes and beliefs', in plain language – starts at the top and cascades down through the organization. So, if the culture is that senior management kicks middle management, then middle management perceives this as the accepted way to behave in this organization and in turn kicks the rest of us. In this way the rest of us learn that kicking and being kicked is the key to status and advancement in the organization.

But think for a minute. Who can the rest of the workforce kick? There's no one left inside the company so, not uncommonly,

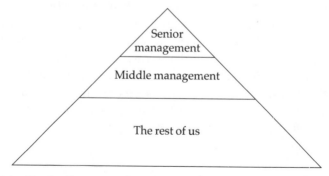

Figure 7.1   Typical organizational structure

they'll look outside. And guess who's first in line. We might more appropriately draw the structure as in Figure 7.2. In this type of transparent organization, if staff are treating customers less

Figure 7.2   Customers in the organization chart

positively than you would like, it may be because of the way they themselves are treated. In these terms, it becomes obvious that your front-line customer contact staff are more than a little disposed to interact with the customers in much the same way as the upper echelons interact with them. *Ergo,* if you want to encourage a higher quality of customer service, the first step is not necessarily hugely expensive training courses. It may be much more effective to examine your corporate culture and ask whether management by its attitudes and actions encourages the standard of service you would like the customers to receive.

Doing it better continues with thoughtfulness
I've spent quite a lot of time in the foregoing pages examining how technology is stimulating ever-rising performance in a whole variety of marketplaces. One area where it has so far threatened to do the opposite is in customer service.

I referred in the case study above to the impression we gained that the bank staff seemed unaware of the number of our accounts held at the branch. Technology allowed them to focus on one, report an overdraft over the limit and write a curt letter at the touch of a button. But because the system had apparently been written for supplier benefit and not customer benefit it evidently could not disclose other circumstances that should have influenced the decision on how to handle the situation.

Of course, technology itself is neutral. It's how it's used that affects supplier–customer relationships. So take this as a plea. If you're writing or commissioning software control systems please take the poor old customer into account. A system that is created wholly from your point of view will not serve you well in a market where customer service yields a distinct competitive advantage.

Doing it better means dealing with individuals as people

It's probably the ultimate truism that people do business with people. This is so to such an extent that you may forget how fragile human beings can be. And nothing ensures a lost customer as much as a bruised ego.

Psychology seems to be playing an ever-increasing part in the world of commerce and business as organizations and individuals seek further afield for that elusive competitive edge. It's not my intention here to examine the benefits that an awareness of psychology can bring to your individual and corporate performance. However, it must be blatantly obvious that we are all drawn to experiences that make us feel better about ourselves and shy away from those that make us feel worse. When I feel that my identity has in some way been acknowledged I warm to the person responsible because I am made to feel that I matter. That's why recovering well from 'physical' errors can often enhance the relationship with the customer, as alluded to above. But do take care here. If this is done in a false way it is very obvious and quickly has the opposite effect.

Thus if you treat a customer so as to diminish him/her in his/her own eyes don't be surprised if he/she stops doing business with you. Some of the more extreme instances of this are obvious. No one with any sense makes a customer feel foolish. But how good are you at putting your customer at ease in the context of your own professional expertise? The garage mechanic who tells me it's obvious that my sprogget-flanges are up the spout and I should have noticed it months ago will not get my business next time. Equally, the solicitor who was condescending in the way she explained the finer points of inheritance law to me did not hear from me again. There are undoubtedly issues over which I shall remain for ever ignorant – that's why I consult garages and solicitors. But I don't want to be belittled when you demonstrate your expertise in front of me.

Interestingly, this has an organizational aspect as well. The employee who is never praised by his manager for good performance may well feel the need to demonstrate superior expertise to the customer. If the motive is to build his own ego rather than to enhance the customer's interests, this will be quickly conveyed by an attitude of superiority. The result is another lost customer. So think about it: how good is your organization at giving praise where praise is due? And what's the effect on your customer relationships if you don't? And how good are you and your staff at dealing with people as people?

Summary

- In commodity markets there are fewer and fewer ways of establishing competitive advantage.
- One of the main areas that remains is the quality of service you offer, as opposed to the physical features of the product or service you supply.
- Whereas we tend to take physical performance for granted, service quality is still noticeably variable throughout the market.
- These service aspects therefore often form a significant part of the customer's buying criteria.
- In some cases service aspects can be more important than the physical features in the perception that the customer forms of your organization. Hence a good recovery from a physical error can enhance the supplier/customer relationship.
- Managing the customer service process starts with management's attitude and culture. You can't expect staff to behave differently towards the customers from how their managers behave towards them.
- You should review your information technology from the

point of view of customer service. Systems are often created with far too little attention to customers.

● Ultimately, the key issue in service provision revolves around relationships between customer and supplier. How good you and your staff are at creating and maintaining relationships and the 'feel-good factor' for the customer will have a deeply significant impact on your level of profitability.

8 Competitor Analysis

If you have taken to heart the quotation from William Bain at the beginning of Part II, you will have already asked yourself some questions about the degree of attention that you pay to what's happening outside your business. I hope that, as you've read this far, you've taken on board the idea that you really do need to know this. If so, you're already in the more perceptive minority, since most people in most companies seem not to pay enough attention to what is happening outside – or if they do they feel powerless to do anything about it.

But what is happening outside is not only a question of customers and strategic market development. We've mentioned a number of times the other guys who are trying to do what you do – the competition.

Some people can only think of the competitive process in a negative frame – it's a dog-eat-dog world / there's only so much to go around and if I want more you get less / I really don't care about you, my concern is only me – and so on. Call me naïve, but I prefer to think of competition as a fundamentally beneficial process. It causes all of us to concentrate harder on what we do in order to do it better and more cost effectively, and to bring new products on stream faster. Seen in that way, competition is good for me and it makes me better at what I do. This is not to say however, that we live in a congenial world where we're all kind to one another and just can't wait to help others. Far from it. The competitive process only works in creating greater efficiency if you act in a self-interested way. So what do you need to know about the competition, how do you go about finding out and what do you do when you have the information?

Competitor analysis – the traditional approach

Again, there is plenty of well-developed theory available on this subject. Most of it talks about profiling particular competitors that you see as significant to you within the context of some sort of market mapping exercise.

This seems fine to me as long as you're ICI or BP, in which case you're one of a relatively small number of powerful players operating in a decidedly imperfect market. You're playing in a multi-player chess game in which each move is analysed by each of the other players to establish its strategic significance. Each move is then pre-empted or responded to appropriately.

But for most of us, life isn't like that. At the risk of sounding like a broken record, we mostly operate in commodity markets where there are large numbers of buyers and sellers. Nevertheless, each of us operating within our chosen markets knows that every other supplier in the market is trying to gain competitive advantage and improve the performance of their business. If the improvement is in the form of an increase in turnover in a relatively low-growth market it means the loss of market share for someone else. If the advantage is efficiency-oriented the result is a new or cheaper product which then attracts more market share. It's the same either way – it just takes a little longer if the advantage is internal.

So, if you want to prevent the other guys gaining the advantage at your expense, there are two things you must do in addition to watching the strategic development of the marketplace. First, you must perpetually innovate (yes that means you, not the high-tech business round the corner – innovation means much more than technology). This is the subject of Chapter 12. Second, you must find out what the competition is doing, either individually if there are significant individual competitors or *en masse* if the general drift or trend of performance is more relevant.

Company D: An exercise in competitor analysis

Some time ago we did some project work with company D, a regional insurance broker of both life and general insurance. The company was making losses and losing market share (but other than that everything was fine!). We were asked to look at the general situation and advise on measures to improve performance.

Company D was unfortunate enough to have lived through the boom of the 1980s. I say unfortunate, because boom brought almost as many problems as recession. In this case it disguised inefficiencies and caused the company to make expansion commitments that would subsequently be difficult to finance. Management information had been limited and management had merrily taken on more staff in departments that were later found to be making a loss. It had not been realized that the company was being shored up by one very high-producing department. Commitments had also been made to long-term leases at rents that in due course seemed astronomic.

The business thus entered the downturn overstaffed, overcommitted and somewhat at a competitive disadvantage. Added to that, strategic change was taking place in certain sectors of the marketplace. And in this case the changes were technologically driven.

As anyone aware of the insurance market knows, the more information you can obtain on a customer base the better your position to judge the degree of risk and quote accordingly. Advances in information technology have progressively meant that insurance companies can hold more and more risk data and offer increasingly competitive quotes to the least risky categories of business. The effect of this at the customer end is that more and more insurance products show characteristics of having arrived at commodity status. Technology makes it easy to provide such products.

Now, if you're an insurance provider looking for more profit, and products are becoming ever easier to provide, you start to wonder why you use brokers at all, since the traditional function of a broker is to deal with complexity and to select among competing products. Thus in the early 1990s insurance providers increasingly wanted to go direct to the customer and cut out the broker. This had all sorts of implications for competition among the insurance providers themselves, but here we were working for a broker. And this particular broker was having to face difficult questions about fundamental inefficiencies in the operation of the business at the same time as the competitive balance in the marketplace was changing.

Looking outside the company, we started with competitor research. We needed to know how customer-friendly the competition was, but that wasn't particularly difficult. The main issue was the generality of competition in the marketplace rather than the positioning of particular competitors, and our enquiries revealed that we definitely had a problem.

It was clear that the drift to direct supply of commodity status insurance products was set to continue for some time to come. Frankly, for simple products it's more efficient. The competitor base seemed to divide into two camps: those that were winning market share through the attraction of commodity business and those that, like our client, were suffering loss of market share and were worrying about it.

We could have mapped this in the traditional competitor analysis format, but this wasn't necessary once we'd perfected the basic framework for considering the competitors. Nevertheless, we had to respond to the competitive pressure somehow. To do so, we went back to first principles and asked ourselves what kind of business we were in. Not the insurance business, as you might first be tempted to think, but the brokerage business. And what were the fundamental services supplied by a broker? Market knowledge, volume purchasing and the lower prices possible as a result (the wholesaling function) and expertise in complexity.

The next question to ask was to which part of the market these services continued to be relevant. Market knowledge isn't the service it used to be. It's very easy for me as customer to obtain quotes from the direct suppliers. Volume purchasing in commodity products has also had its day in the light of direct-supply advantages. However, not all insurance products have yet taken on the characteristics of commodity status – some still require expertise, especially commercial insurances. So, the logic went, if company D wanted to continue to supply expertise, it had to find a market where that service was still relevant – the commercial market.

It would take time to develop significantly more business in the commercial market than they currently undertook. What would happen in the meantime? Fortunately for this company they had a niche within one of the commodity markets that the major players had still not spotted. They marketed a branded insurance product to a sector of the commodity market where risk was low and price could be quoted correspondingly lower. And the fact that their low-priced products attracted enquiries also had associated benefits for their other products. However, company D realized that this niche was no more than a window of opportunity where they would have competitive advantage for a while but not for ever. The strategy was therefore to concentrate on the niche as a cash cow for as long as it offered good returns and to apply the income so generated to the development of the problem child commercial product range.

It worked; but only because the company developed a good understanding of the competitor base that they were up against. While others were wringing their hands and adopting me-too strategies, attempting to compete in a market where they were fundamentally at a disadvantage, company D had read the market correctly and was on its way to a new strategic direction for the business.

The competition – what do you need to know?

Knowledge of the competition is important, especially in the strategy that you develop for your own business. So what do you need to know? This is a 'piece of string' question. You need to know about those factors that make for competitive advantage in your marketplace. Some of the factors are internally focused, to do with the efficiency of an operation. Others have an external focus, to do with how well competitors are reading the requirements of the market and addressing them.

As far as the internal side of the equation is concerned, you need to take a long hard look at *your own* production processes, information and other systems and ask if they're really delivering what they should as efficiently as they should – the subject of Part III. If they're not, you'll be placed at a perpetual disadvantage in respect of the competition, shored up only by the knowledge that most organizations' internal operations fall well short of their efficiency potential.

Why look inside for competitive analysis? Answer, because it's hard to gain this information about the competition. You can see quite easily what they are doing in the market – such information is in the public domain. But internally, it's safer to start with the assumption that the market leaders, or at least the key competitors, are as efficient as they possibly can be, so you need to be too. Add to that such cost data as are available through the likes of filed accounts (but watch the time lag) and credit ratings, and you can begin to form a picture of the main factors that make for internal efficiency.

As far as the outside world is concerned, let me reiterate that for most of us the issue is not the behaviour of a particular competitor, but the behaviour of the generic category 'competitor' or 'supplier'. If that's not true for you and there is a key competitor you're interested in, simply apply the following thoughts to that supplier. But for most of us the thinking applies to the market in general.

You need to formulate a model of how your own competitive marketplace operates. In the case of company D above we formulated a competitive model of the insurance broking market. This is merely a high-sounding way of saying that we isolated the key issues that were important to competitive performance. These will vary from one industry to another. To identify yours think again about what your business is. What customer needs does your company truly supply? These are the reasons why you exist as an organization.

When you have identified those issues, ask yourself how other organizations are addressing the supply of those services. Are any doing particularly well (or badly) in your marketplace? Are any new entrants bringing in thinking or technology that have been applied successfully elsewhere? Is there anything being done – or that could be done – to render the delivery of these key services or products more effective? Is there any communication mechanism, or any association of your product with another that would make your product more attractive *vis-à-vis* competitor products?

In short, the essence of commodity competitor analysis is the most basic form of questioning that you can undertake – what do we actually do? If you look around the commodity marketplaces you will find that the development of competitive advantage has often been achieved by re-examining fundamental questions that most people consider too blindingly obvious to be worth reassessing.

The competition – specific issues

Once again, the specific issues you should consider will vary from case to case. I would begin by taking a broad perspective on my marketplace. Do you see yourself operating in a global market? A national market? A regional market? All three?

Who are the significant competitors? Specific individual players or many small ones? If they are the latter, do they divide into logical categories or identifiable market sub-sectors? If your business is fast food, at one level you might be interested in the general direction fast food is taking nationally, the number of suppliers in your area and the number of closely analogous suppliers in each relevant locality.

What are the competitors doing? Are new entrants coming into the market daily? Are they deserting the market because of underprofitability? Are they expanding the number of outlets? Do they tend to be single-outlet businesses? Are large corporates dominant in the market or is it fragmented into many small suppliers? All these issues have a bearing on where the market generally and individual competitors are going.

How good are the competitors? What is the standard of performance – in terms of both product and customer service – of the supplier base generally and of any significant competitors in particular? Does anyone have a superior product to your own? Is anyone addressing a market sub-sector that is noticeably more attractive than your own? Is anyone attracting business through superior customer service?

If you're consistently (and realistically) coming up with the answer that you're better than the field, congratulations. But how do you make sure you maintain your market lead? Is anyone catching you up? What have you learned from the market about customer preference and where is there room for any improvement in what you do?

The competition – how do you find out?

Some markets are easy to observe and competitive data simply drop into your hands. Generally, any activity with a prominent public face – e.g. retail – is relatively easy to track. It's not difficult to walk into someone else's restaurant or shopping mall and observe the product/service characteristics. Do it often enough round the country and you can begin to build up a picture of their competitive strategy quite easily. The situation is more difficult in the less visible trades. How do you track the activities, strategy and intentions of an office supply operation? A training company? A software house? An architectural practice?

Here you have a choice of two directions. Either you must enquire under-the-counter – the morality of which you may have doubts about – or you take the overall market perspective. At this level I would tend to research public domain data as thoroughly as possible – industry reports, professional association magazines, local industry gossip and so on. I would also spend some time talking to customers about the competition and how well I measured up against it. Customers are often also customers of other suppliers and I consider it wholly legitimate to enquire into my customers' perceptions of my operation and its strengths and weaknesses compared to other suppliers of the same product or service.

I usually find that it's not too hard to build up a picture of what the key issues are in a given industry. And at that point I can ask myself if I really do need detailed information on Sprogget & Co. in particular. The answer is usually that I don't – beyond what's already in the public domain.

The competition – what to do when you know

By this time you've undertaken all the research you can, formally and anecdotally, and you have a great deal of data in your hands. It's time to turn those data into useful information. All this is only to your benefit if you use the information to re-examine your current practices and strategy and modify them where appropriate. Start by asking yourself the following:

- What key developments are taking place in my industry now? These might be related to the emergence of new products or customers, new entrants into the market or new technology for the product. What can I learn and do differently?
- What are other players doing that I am not, and vice versa? What can I learn and do differently?
- What key competitive advantages do I perceive either my own business or competitors to have? What benefit do such advantages yield? How effectively are the firms concerned exploiting them? What can I learn and do differently?
- What do I think will happen in this industry in the foreseeable future? How well am I and other suppliers positioned to take best advantage of the changes? What can I learn and do differently?
- Have there been any failures amongst competitors? Why did they occur? How do I avoid following the same route?

This leads you towards some questions of overriding importance. They are:

1   What are the key performance criteria in this business, i.e. what are the factors that make the difference between success and failure?
2   Who has taken best advantage of these criteria and how have they done it?
3   How do I compare in the light of the performance criteria I have identified?
4   Am I succeeding by my own estimation?
5   Will I continue to do so, given the changes I think will take place in the foreseeable future?

It should be obvious by now that at least some of the answers to these questions involve internal aspects of the performance of your business. It is to these internal considerations we turn in the next part.

Summary

- Competitor analysis in the commodity market deals at least as much with the generality of competition as with isolating and investigating specific competitors.
- Start by formulating your own view – a model, if you wish – of how your marketplace operates. What are the key considerations in the environment in which you function?
- The specific issues you should take into account will vary from market to market, but there are some common factors.
- Start by looking internally. Identify the factors that are relevant to your own performance, and you'll probably also have identified those that are significant to competitors' performance.
- Draw on as much public domain data as you can – filed accounts, industry reports as well as feedback from your own customers.
- Use the information you glean to specify the main issues and trends that are affecting your market now and those that are likely to become relevant in the future.
- Rate your performance against the competition generally and

against any outstanding performers. Find out why others are doing better or worse and allow your conclusions to influence the way you run your business.

- Become aware of the questions that are most significant to the performance of your business – the key performance criteria. Then make a realistic assessment of how well you are performing in that context.

Part III
Under the Microscope

. . . it seemed to me that every time we were beginning to form up into teams we would be reorganised. I was to learn later in life that we tend to meet any new situation by reo rganising, and a wonderful method it can be for creating the illusion of progress while p roducing confusion, inefficiency and demoralisation.

Petronius Arbiter (A.D. 65)

Map of the model

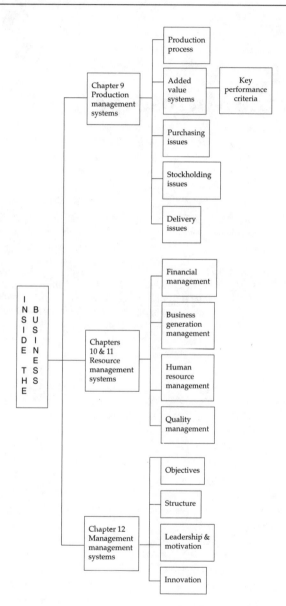

9 Production Management Systems

The main theme of the argument so far is that it's possible to categorize all factors that influence the profitability of your business within three areas:

1 The outside world, which on the whole you can't control, only react to. But if you react with understanding and sympathetically you can make the best of the circumstances you are presented with.
2 The communication process between you and the outside world, which is at least partially under your control, despite the fact that many organizations behave as if it weren't.
3 The means by which you manage and control what you do inside the business, which is decidedly under your control and the importance of which a great number of organizations have still not realized.

This final part of *How to Make More Profit* concentrates on the third of these areas: what is happening within your business.

If you glance at the chapter headings in Part III, you'll see that we're essentially examining system issues. For many organizations, this will be the first point at which we part company: for many businesses, the concept of systematization is alien. It's still very common to find that an organization operates largely by fire-fighting, always in a crisis, never quite getting in control.

This approach is detrimental to the interests of both customers and the business itself since it increases the risks of customer dissatisfaction and also reduces profit. Typical excuses for management by fire-fighting are: 'We have to be very responsive to short-notice demands from our customers' or 'All our work is unique project work. No two projects are the same, so we can't create a system'. Now at the risk of getting shot at by many former clients, I don't believe these excuses hold water. Any business that can be said to be in the business of 'X-ing' (whatever X may be) is also susceptible to a significant degree of systematic control, if for no other reason than because X-ing is an activity consistent enough to be identifiable in itself. You are not unique – other people also do what you do. You do not (usually) do it uniquely for one customer. You do it for several, and there is at least a certain similarity among the services you provide to each.

Lack of system is normally symptomatic of sloppy thinking and nothing else. If you don't subscribe to that view, you may not want to continue reading – but then you'd miss all the good things that are coming. So at least humour me for a little while.

Production management – what do we mean?

I want to make clear what is meant by production management in this context. Many fine manufacturing and production control systems exist, but that's not the point here. Production here means the whole process by which you create and deliver your product or service to the customer – all the sequential activities that make the coal dust into diamonds and deliver them to the customer – or whatever it is that you do do. But note that for present purposes, until it's in the customer's hands it isn't fully produced.

It's instructional (and often particularly so for larger companies) to take a step back and map the whole of the business process. People in big organizations often lose sight of the wood for the trees in terms of what actually happens within the various departments of their business. If you take the time to map the big picture you begin to see how to control the whole process rather than just its constituent parts. Think of it in terms of Figure 9.1.

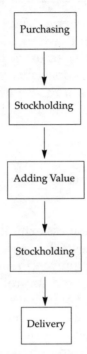

Figure 9.1   The production process

This is nonsense, you may say; our business is far more compli-cated than that. Well, if you leave out all the items to do with managing the resources and processes (which we'll come to later), exactly what do you do that can't be fitted into this model? Indeed, you may have nothing of significance happening in some of the boxes, especially if you're a service operation, which is fine for present purposes. But I doubt if there's anything of significance happening in the production process that doesn't fit into one of the categories. This is important because it allows us to categorize and therefore systematize and hence *render subject to control* the various consequential activities that take place within your business.

Adding value

Apparently somewhat perversely, I want to start in the middle of this process with what I've termed 'adding value'. Think of it, if you will, as the creative part of the process, where your organization does whatever it is specialist at. And at this stage I'd like to suggest that there is a limited number of categories into which adding-value activities can be subdivided. In my map of the world there are three:

1 Facility providers
2 Widget manufacturers
3 Project managers.

It may be that your business exhibits characteristics of more than one of these categories. The reason for examining these categories is that the *key performance criteria* (the most important variables for measurement and control) for each are different. If you can see which category of business you fall into and identify the key performance criteria for that category, it becomes much easier to see what the overriding issues are for you. It then becomes clearer what you should concentrate on controlling. The production management system that you then develop and utilize should be built around the key performance criteria for your type of business.

Facility providers

The type of businesses concerned here are those that provide some kind of facility for others to use. Typical of the category are airlines, hotels, care homes, warehouses. Businesses of this nature usually face high fixed costs associated with providing the facility they offer. The key to profitability in these cases is *utilization* – the extent to which the facility is in fact used – say occupancy per night or year for a hotel, occupancy per aircraft for an airline. The break-even level of turnover will often be fairly high, but normally turnover beyond the break-even level will be very profitable. The reason is simple. A minimum level of turnover is needed to cover the high fixed costs. But when those costs have been covered, the variable cost – the incremental cost of providing the service – is relatively low. Beyond the break-even point, the marginal revenue contributed by each unit sold can be extremely high (see Chapter 10 below for further details on break-even analysis).

The problem with businesses of this nature is that everyone else in the industry also faces high fixed costs. This is fine so long as demand is buoyant. But when demand falls – say in a recession – reducing capacity within the industry is often very painful or difficult. And because everyone else is trying to stay alive as well, the result is usually that the whole industry experiences under-utilization of capacity. And the problem with under-utilization in businesses with high fixed costs is that it translates very quickly into substantial losses. Both the hotel and airline industries have experienced this problem extensively in the early 1990s. Whether you can sustain a loss position for very long depends significantly on the level of gearing (loan and equity capital) you have in place (for more on this see Chapter 10).

So, if you're in the facility provision business the key performance criterion will be utilization. And how you maximize that primarily concerns sales, marketing and customer service as dealt with in the sections above. If you are in this position, stop for a moment and ask yourself exactly how good you are at the business generation process itself and how much attention you are paying to your key performance criteria. Is your management information system built around it? Do all the hotels return occupancy rates daily? Is there anything to be learned from the high sales profile industries in terms of how sales are generated? What is the level of customer service like – not just from the little leaflets you leave in everyone's rooms, but what is it like to be a customer of your organization? If you don't know, find out.

All this is not to say that utilization and sales turnover are the only figures you need to keep your eye on. But in this type of business it appears to me that they are the most important – the ones that lead to the success or failure of every other measure and eventually the business itself. 'Production' management in this context should focus on utilization; everything else should be allowed to emanate from this.

Widget manufacturers

I've often wondered where the term 'widget' originates. Presumably there was once a product called a widget but the term has now passed into the folklore of business language. The issue here is that there is a very large category of value-added activity that is wholly or largely standardized. Whether you're producing cans of beans or dry-cleaning suits or selling books, large groups of the product are to all intents and purposes exactly the same. If you're in this position you will typically be selling large numbers of (probably) low-value items, and usually doing it from a price list (with a suitable range of discounts for volume and favoured-status customers). Here the main issues are:

- the total volume you produce and sell;
- the unit gross margin per item that you achieve;
- the level of overheads you carry.

Now factory managers everywhere will be reaching for pens and telephones to tell me that the situation is much more complex than that. There certainly can be many levels within an organization at which you need to measure your key performance criteria. You will sensibly want to know volume and margin per product, per production line, profit before and after factory overhead, performance per subsidiary company and (if relevant) per country. All of which can serve to complicate the matter to the point of uselessness unless you're clear about what you're trying to control.

Part of the solution is to ensure that you have somebody responsible for every identifiable performance criterion that you deem to be significant at each level in the organization at which it is worth measuring. We'll be examining organizational structure and human resource (HR) management in more detail in Chapter 11. But for now, if you're in a standardized production environment and you're losing sight of the wood for all those trees growing on the accountants' spreadsheets, go back to basics. Is there any more important issue at the operational control level than volume, margin and overhead? It's unlikely. As part of the question of key performance criteria, consider the following questions:

- How efficient is your production layout? We once worked with a food-producing company whose production layout itself looked like spaghetti. Every inefficiency in the production process costs you money. When was the last time you looked at it?
- How modern is your production technology? One of the great diseases of the UK manufacturing sector used to be outdated production technology. Mercifully, it seems to be improving but we still come across companies using technology that places them at a competitive disadvantage, particularly against the foreign competition. Outdated equipment tends to have two effects:

  – it breaks down, interferes with production schedules and takes repair time and cost;
  – it typically utilizes more labour time per unit output than does more modern technology.

  Both factors cost you money. Are you aware how much?
- How well coordinated is production with sales? If it's badly coordinated you may be spending too much on finished goods inventory. On the other hand, if you need to produce batches of a minimum efficient size you may have to take a fluctuating inventory cost into account (see the section on stockholding later in this chapter).
- How diverse is the production process? In Part I we examined the trend towards market niches and specialization in smaller and smaller segments of the market. As noted there, the process is largely efficiency-driven; it is often possible to increase efficiency by concentrating on a small range of activities. Much the same is at issue here. We came across a company some time ago that was undertaking numerous

different types of production (all relatively small-volume) which would have been much better undertaken out of house by subcontractors. When was the last time you assessed the degree to which your production process specializes?

A tale of two companies

A couple of stories come to mind that illustrate some of the preceding control and information points vividly.

Company E is in food production (on days when I'm feeling less euphemistic, I tell people that, in reality, they run a group of abattoirs). As anyone from the livestock industry will know, the profitability of what you do is fundamentally dependent on the price at which you buy at market compared to the price at which you send the meat out from the chill room. In fact, in these circles they talk about the 'fifth quarter' – essentially representing the margin per unit of output.

When we were invited to become involved, company E was considering a series of issues ranging from management succession to acquisition of competitors. In addition, we examined the management control system and the information system linked to it. We couldn't find a computer anywhere on site (and this was no small business), but the owner could tell me on a weekly basis how his key performance indicators were moving, what his volume throughput had been, what it had been on the same week for each of the last five years, what margin they had achieved that week and what the overall year-to-date profit was. And he could do it for each of the four production units he owned. Although this wasn't the way I would have monitored performance, I had to admit that he was one of the best-informed business owners I had ever come across. Needless to say, his profit history was extremely impressive.

By contrast, company F was a component manufacturer, with one of the most impressive computer rooms you could ever want to visit – all clicks and whirrs and spreadsheets and printouts. The problem was that all this produced too much data – and not enough usable information. Every month the board (which had 12 members) received a pack of information capable of filling a small fork lift truck. The accountants could point proudly to almost any figure you could conceivably ask for. . . but no one could tell me why the business was underperforming.

Eventually we took the management information system apart and put it back together in a much simpler format that highlighted the key performance criteria – margin and contribution per production unit and per management unit much along the lines outlined above. We ended up with perhaps a page of key performance information per month. It was then easy to pinpoint where the underperformances were taking place, isolate the causes and act appropriately.

Sometimes less really is more.

Project managers

The final category of added-value activity applies to any organization that undertakes bespoke work, where on the whole each item produced is somewhat different. Typically such an organization draws together a number of different elements in the execution of each 'project', such as in the construction industry. The concept can also be usefully applied to organizations that offer a single resource, but deploy it in the achievement of different objectives for each customer. Examples are suppliers of professional services – solicitors, architects, consultants of various kinds.

The differentiating factor lies in the differences among the 'units of output' – or projects that the organization undertakes. Because each item is different, you can't sensibly expect each to contribute equally to the profit of the organization. So how do you measure and control performance? The answer is 'project by project'.

There are normally three key performance criteria for a project:

1 Deadline
2 Quality
3 Cost.

And the big, big problem that often arises in the project management environment but doesn't seem to be nearly as common elsewhere is this: in concentrating on the customer's interests in the project, people lose sight of their own interests.

I'm not suggesting that the customer's interests are not paramount – only that he should be paying for what he's getting. Projects are often enshrined in fixed-price quotations. But in some industries the supplying organization is not nearly good enough at specifying the extent of service that will be provided for the fixed cost. And without a tight specification the temptation is to bend over backwards to please the client, even well beyond the limits of the performance the contract would have specified if it had been tight.

Alternatively it may be that the contract is so tightly drawn that the supplier uses it as a weapon to extract more and more from the customer. Some industries – subcontracting in the construction industry is one example – have turned this almost into an art form. The corresponding argument is usually along the lines of, 'Unless we deal with the contract in this way we make no profit'. I think that in the end everyone's a loser in this kind of situation. The balance lies somewhere in the middle – show goodwill towards the customer but don't overdo it.

So let's look a little more closely at these key performance criteria. First, *deadline* is a key consideration because the unit of output has normally been promised by a specific date. This is very clear in the case of a construction project but commonly equally important in professional services. It's the consideration that, I have found, most suppliers get right, because it's obvious. The project is either delivered on time or it's not. Second, *quality*, which, although less obvious, is nevertheless not normally too much of a problem to most companies in the project management environment. Most organizations (possibly a dangerous generalization) have a reasonable degree of competence in what they do, or they wouldn't be doing it in the first place. If this is a problem in your company, think about some of the issues raised in Chapter 11 below. Third, *cost control* is the most common problem we encounter. In this context we're not talking about the cost the customer pays for the project (which presumably has been specified from the outset by number or by means of calculation) but the cost that you as supplier face in delivering the project by the specified date to the specified quality.

The most common problem is failure to perceive the level of

allowable cost from the start and/or failure to control the expenditure of resource during the life of the project. In some industries (for example construction professions, such as architects or engineers) it's tradition to specify project costs as a percentage of the overall cost of the delivered product. In such cases, the supplier will then sometimes fail to translate the level of income the project is going to deliver into the allowable level of resource expenditure for the project – in this case the number of man hours or days available. Further, even if the total resource level is specified it is often not subdivided into sufficiently small controllable segments to ensure that overruns do not occur. Construction professionals will often say something like, 'Well, we can't just leave the project half-way through simply because we don't have enough time left in the budget'. What this line of argument fails to appreciate is that the performance failure has already taken place before the budget runs out. It occurred when you expended too much resource in the early stages of the project and failed to reserve sufficient for the later stages.

To come back to the centre of the argument, what are the key performance criteria in project management cost control and how do you control them? The overriding issue here is resource cost and volume in comparison with the specified price for the project. I know of no other way to control these variables than to specify a detailed budget for each job and monitor the devotion of resource volume and cost to the project in comparison with the budget. How detailed that budget should be depends very much on your specific circumstances. But to continue with the construction professional example above, I would advocate budgeting at two levels. First, calculate the allowable level of resource from the agreed project price. Then subdivide it into the main categories of activity you know will need to take place (noting that your agreed payment schedule may well not be in proportion to the volume of resource you can reasonably expect to expend at each stage). Then subdivide each category into more meaningful and controllable segments – perhaps the number of drawings anticipated and the man hours available at each stage of the project.

There are then two other elements in successfully managing the project:

- You must monitor the expenditure of resource in comparison with budget throughout the life of the project.
- Someone in the organization must take responsibility for the project – a project manager, if the term is acceptable in your organization.

As far as the first of these is concerned, I have found that unless there is accountability there is no control. Projects must be controlled and reported individually and regularly to a higher authority. As far as the second is concerned, we often find that where a project passes through several departments within a single organization more emphasis is placed on resource management than on project management. The result can be very well controlled resource departments and very badly controlled projects.

Company F, for example, was a full service manufacturer, specializing in small batch production of items for the advertising and promotions industry. Their service ran from initial design, through production of a mock-up, through tooling and on to several production departments and stockholding for customer call-off. Which departments a project passed through depended on the exact nature of the customer specification.

The company was managed very closely by departmental budget – but it had no project managers. The sales department would specify the price for the project in negotiation with the customer. The project would then be passed from department to department, the head of each department taking responsibility for the project in turn. Not surprisingly, projects frequently emerged well over budget and late – largely because although F looked after resources no one in the company cherished the projects.

The solution was to put in a project management team (by redeployment rather than new staff appointments) that managed the projects through the various departments. The almost instant result was a marked increase in the number of projects delivered on time and to budget.

Refer to Figure 9.1 on page 125 and you'll see that we've considered the 'added-value' part of the diagram in the context of the three types of production processes. Remember that we're trying to identify the main influences on your profit inherent in the way you run the internal aspects of your business. To complete the picture, we now turn to purchasing, stockholding and delivery.

Purchasing

Chapter 7 dealt with the subject of customer service, the interface between the organization and its customers. In an exactly analogous way, the purchasing function is the interface between the business and its suppliers. And in the same way that we examined customer service if the customer relationship needs to be enhanced, so we can attend to purchasing if the supplier relationship is delivering less than it could.

Purchasing is one of those areas in which we find that the experiences and problems of large organizations differ greatly from those of small organizations. That said, we come across companies at both ends of the scale whose purchasing functions are extremely well organized and others who apparently have never heard of the word.

Big-company issues
In large organizations the last ten years or so have seen a continuing drift towards much greater departmental and personal accountability for financial performance. One of the consequences of this is that more people operate under budgets and fewer resources are provided by the organization to budgetholders 'free'. Thus, in general we find that in big companies more and more resources are rendered subject to control.

One interesting example of this relates to an extremely large PLC we worked with some time ago. As in many big organizations, its operating subsidiaries were individually accounted for, but were provided with central facilities including office space, print, site services and so on. A new facilities director was appointed, charged with the responsibility of reducing central overhead. His strategy was straightforward. He worked on the principle that if people have to pay for something they tend to value it more than if it's provided free, or by way of departmental levy. So he simply started charging for as many of the central services as possible. And as time went by it proved to be possible to charge user departments for more and more of the central services on a pure utilization basis. You may argue that this merely amounted to moving the deckchairs around, since the services had to be paid for somehow. That was true to some extent. But what was most interesting was the number of services – and in one case a whole department – that the organization could dispense with on the basis that when charged, nobody was actually willing to buy.

On the other side of the coin, one of the most common purchasing problems we encounter in large organizations concerns the degree of centralization that is appropriate. If you centralize purchasing you can find that you create a slow-moving bureaucracy that misses opportunities and special local deals. Without centralized control over purchasing you may fail to take the best advantage of your buying power. The right balance needs to be struck organization by organization.

On a related note, it is also fairly common to come across large organizations that use their buying power so excessively (over credit terms, price etc.) that it becomes virtually impossible for small organizations to deal with them. In this kind of case the big customer may think it is winning, but in reality both potential supplier and potential customer miss the benefits that could have been available. Such organizations may like to take note of the quality of relationship and service that can be generated by referring to the case study quoted in the section of Chapter 10 on 'Balance sheet management – Creditors'.

Small-company issues

The main problem we encounter in small organizations is that management is too busy doing something else to spend time purchasing effectively. Naturally, attention is concentrated on output and sales and frequently purchasing comes a poor third if it gets a look-in at all. If you're in this position it is best to look at your spending pattern periodically. For production-related purchases you probably do this anyway, since it is one of the components of your gross margin, but you need to do the same for overhead expenditure as well. Ask yourself whether you need to make a particular expenditure at all. We tend to become so used to doing the same thing in the same way that we fail to appreciate whether purchases are necessary or not. If you're satisfied that there is a need to buy, ask yourself if there is a more effective way of buying, for example:

- Reduced list of approved suppliers?
- Less frequent spends in larger quantities?
- Committed spend with a call-off over a period of time?
- Retrospective discounts with key suppliers based on amount spent?

Very often the savings are there for the taking – if only you take the time to look for them.

Stockholding

There are just a few main points to raise here and they all start with one question:

- Do you know what it is costing you to hold stock?

It's a salutary lesson to calculate your stockholding cost; such an exercise can help to reduce it if it is significant (for more on this see Chapter 10).

Here, too, there is often a distinction between small and large companies. It's much more common to find good stock control systems in large companies than in small ones. But whether you're large or small, the key to minimizing stockholding costs is the ability to coordinate production with purchases and sales. Close monitoring of the level of production you expect to undertake has direct implications for the level of stock you need to carry. The less control you have over production and the longer the lead-time for input stock, the larger the volume of purchased stock you have to hold. At the other end of the process the same is largely true. The more certainty you have as to the level of supply you must maintain, the lower the finished goods inventory you will need to carry, because you can scale production to fit in with your customers' delivery requirements.

At this point, you can almost hear the response: 'We don't have any influence over when our customers call for supply so we have to hold high stocks at both ends of the production process'. Maybe . . . but maybe not. You're only justified in taking this view if you have actually looked into the issue. Consider:

- When was the last time you spoke to suppliers and customers about the issue of delivery and call-off? There may be a way to alter how you manage the relationship to the advantage of both sides. If your customer can tell you in advance what his/her requirements will be, it saves you cost. Perhaps you can pass some of the savings on to him/her.
- If you sell to end customers, how much information do you record month by month, year by year on sales pattern and what determines them?
- What would be the cost of running out of stock and losing a sale compared to the cost of holding stock? The answer may not be as obvious as you may at first think.
- How much do you lose annually through deterioration and write-off of stock? If you permit stock to become obsolete or unusable the cost can become phenomenal.

If this section has done nothing else, I trust it has caused you to think about the costs you are incurring in a rather Cinderella-like area of the business – but one that can genuinely help you to make more profit.

Delivery

How, then, do you get goods to the customer? If you don't need to because the customer comes to you, smile smugly and move on. If you do deliver or distribute in some fashion, once again there is a cost involved and that cost is as susceptible to management and control as any other part of your operation.

We often come across distribution systems which on the face of it could be rendered far more efficient by making changes – less frequent delivery, for example. But commonly this can't be done because the customer requires a frequency of delivery that the supplier must adhere to if he wants to keep the business. The consequence of this is inefficient delivery rosters which management knows about but cannot change.

The key to cost minimization in delivery is volume. An excellent demonstration of this took place some years ago when the big UK supermarkets transferred from a local to a centralized delivery system. Handling much larger volumes combined with electronic point of sale monitoring has permitted an immense improvement in delivery and stockholding efficiency.

Even if you're not an enormous grocery retailer, there are still lessons to be learned from this guiding principle. Maybe none of them will apply to your unique circumstances. However, do make the appropriate investigation before you write them off. Ask yourself the following questions:

- Should you be delivering at all? If your production volume is relatively small and you deliver over a relatively large area it may be more cost-effective to subcontract delivery. Remember what we've said in numerous places about specialization and efficiency. When you take into account the labour costs of delivery, running and depreciation costs on vehicles etc., it may pay you to let someone else do the work.
- Can you concentrate your sales activities in particular areas so as to raise volumes in those areas and make delivery costs more effective?
- Is there something you can work out with the customer to make larger, less frequent deliveries work for both of you?
- Can the delivery process be subdivided into more than one step, using local warehousing from which customer call-off is undertaken?

Summary

We've covered a great deal of ground in this chapter and clearly not exhausted the subject. I hope, however, that it has been enough to tickle your thinking and help you to identify where in the production process you can make more profit. The key points we've examined are as follows:

- Production processes can be subdivided into the sequential steps of getting purchases turned into products and delivered to the customer. They can also be subdivided by the type of added-value service being undertaken, facility provision, widget production and project management being the most common categories.
- The key performance criteria vary among the different types of added-value activity; it's important to identify those that you apply to for your type of business.
- If your business is to provide a facility, the critical issues revolve around utilization of that facility. Your performance management systems need to concentrate on these issues. If you're in widget production, the issues lie in the interrelationship between volume, margin and overhead. For project managers the matters to attend to first and foremost are deadline, quality and cost control. All this is not to say that you can ignore the issues relevant to other business types than your own – only that you must be aware of the main determinants of performance in your type of operation.
- Regardless of the type of business, the earlier and later stages in the production process are also susceptible to much closer management than many give them credit for – purchasing, stockholding and delivery. Consider carefully the issues raised, because each function can have a significant impact on profit.

10 Resource Management Systems – the Big Picture

I make no apology for the fact that most of this chapter will be devoted to the subject of financial management. In one sense the whole process of business management amounts to resource management, since you are in the business of applying resources to the meeting of customer needs, whether you produce products or services. The extent to which you make a profit depends to a very large extent on the effectiveness and efficiency with which you control the application of resource to the meeting of need – and in the end that's financially measurable.

Resource management means utilizing the resources that are available to you in the most effective way to achieve the outcomes that you want for your business. This book assumes that the purpose of the business is to maximize profit, but within that objective you devote resources to the achievement of sub-goals along the way. Some resources you devote to the generation of business; some you devote to the execution of business – producing the output that you sell. Some of those resources will be inanimate, some human. The exact spread will depend on what your business is. But the following are the most common resources and means of deployment that need management:

1   Resources

- human resources
- material resources.

2   Deployment systems

- business generation
- business execution
- quality management.

Individual businesses will have many other resources and processes that need to be managed but the above are the most common that we encounter.

Each of the processes in which you engage with a view to creating profit needs management. Each of the resources that you deploy in the pursuit of your objectives needs management. The purpose of managing both resources and processes is to maximize efficiency and effectiveness. So a question arises:

- To what extent does your business manage the resources and systems it utilizes?

The answer to this question determines, perhaps more than anything else, the extent to which you are maximizing profit, or the achievement of any other objective you care to set for the business. Each of the above categories needs to have an identifiable system in place for its management. Also the business as a whole needs a summary management system that allows you to monitor and manipulate its financial performance.

Resource management overview: the management of financial performance

The purpose of a financial management system is to tell you how well the business is performing. Once again, I suggest that the system you need to employ for financial management of the business should revolve around the concept of key performance criteria. There are certain performance elements that are much more significant to your business objectives than others. Concentrate primarily on these and you will be prioritizing the most important aspects of the business.

The accountancy profession has made almost an art form of the heights of complexity that financial management can rise to and the degree of detail it can involve. However, I'd like to suggest that there is a fairly limited number of concepts that you should focus on in evaluating the performance of your business. These are:

1   The budget.
2   Profit and loss items:

- turnover
- gross margin
- overhead
- net profit.

3   Balance sheet items:

- liquidity
- speed of cash collection
- level of working capital (primarily stocks, work in progress, debtors).

4   Analytical items:

- key ratios
- the break-even point.

If you can focus your attention on these items at the various levels within the business at which performance matters most, you will be able to isolate the issues that contribute most significantly to the overall performance of the business.

Let's take an example to see how this works in practice. Company G is a manufacturing concern that operates in three

countries. In each country it has a number of operating subsidiary companies and each operating subsidiary has a number
of plants. What we therefore have here is a number of operating
units and a number of different levels within the business at
which decisions are made in pursuit of the business's objective –
the maximization of long-term profit.

Budgets

First and foremost, I would expect to see company G set a budget
detailing anticipated financial performance at each of the decision-making levels within the organization. It is for the company
itself to decide what the decision-making levels are (some
thoughts on how you structure organizations appear in Chapter
12) but in a case like this I would expect budgeting to take place
at operating unit, subsidiary, national and company level.

We find that there are two common problems in the budgeting
process: those organizations that still operate without a budget
and those that base them on last year's performance. As far as
the former is concerned, this is often the case in a small company.
My only comment here would be to ask how, if you don't lay
down expectations of performance, do you know whether your
organization is doing as well as it can? Maybe, if you're the only
decision-maker within the business, you can manage to carry
some of this in your head. But as soon as it gets just a little bigger
or as soon as others participate in decision-making you're going
to need to disclose your expectations if you want others to perform according to them.

The latter point – setting budgets based on last year's performance – raises some quite interesting questions on the issue of
how budgets should be set. The biggest problem that I encounter
in larger companies is that subsidiaries often set budgets to satisfy the demands of higher management, whilst giving a minimum of thought to the purpose of setting them in the first place.

Go back to basics for a moment. In my opinion, the most
important purpose of the budget is to give you a yardstick by
which to judge performance. You may argue that if your budget
is based on last year plus 5 per cent, you might as well simply use
last year's figures as the budget for this year. However, a budget

needs to be much more thoughtfully composed than this implies. You should re-examine from the ground up what it is possible for your organization to achieve. That means taking a periodic look at the factors that influence performance:

- What will the market environment permit you to do this year?
- What capacity utilization does this imply?
- How could you increase capacity utilization?
- How could you increase labour efficiency?

Ask these questions each time you create a budget.

Whatever method you choose, we'll now assume that you've put your budget together. We're then left with two tasks: managing the profit flow of the business (profit and loss account); and managing the financial strength, stability and liquidity of the business (balance sheet). I know of no other sensible way of doing this than through periodic management accounts.

Management accounting

The purpose of producing management accounting information is to enable you to monitor whether you are on target to expectations and to act quickly in the event of any deviation.

Questions that arise here are how often should such information be produced, how accurate should it be and how quickly should it be produced? Each question needs to be answered specifically in the context of your own business. Some organizations need to collect data daily or even hourly. But at the level of management accounting I would start to get uneasy in any situation where more than a month was allowed to elapse without the production of summary management information.

As regards accuracy and speed of production, there is usually a trade-off here. The faster you want the information, the more risks you take over its accuracy. On the one hand, there's not much point in producing information so late that it cannot be acted upon. On the other hand, it's dangerous to take action based on information that you know could be seriously flawed. As a rule of thumb (and please note it's no more than that) I normally look for monthly management control information to be produced within ten working days of the month end. And I expect that information to be divided into profit and loss information and balance sheet information.

Profit and loss management

Given a reasonably sophisticated information technology system most organizations of any size can these days produce full profit and loss accounts and balance sheets against budget. Great. But what do you do with the information once obtained? It's often the very complexity of the information produced that gives rise to problems. Giving people too much information is almost as bad as not giving them enough – they can't see the wood for the trees.

Therefore, even if the system is capable of telling you to the penny what the cleaning budget was by square footage in offices A to Z, it's usually better, at least initially, to stand back and look at information in summary format. If this perspective then indicates some kind of problem, you can investigate in more depth through your super-duper knobs and whistles accounting system.

At summary level these are the most important questions to be asking:

- Did we achieve the turnover we expected?
- Did we achieve the gross margin we expected?
- Did we incur the total overhead we expected?
- Did we make the profit we expected?

In each case, if the information system indicates that you did not get what you expected, that's the time to delve further. If turnover was not what was expected, which products deviated? Which sales teams? Which regions? What were the reasons and what action is open to you to correct or compensate for the position? But all those questions come after the overview examination and not before it.

Balance sheet management

It is common in our high-technology age to find detailed balance sheet accounting in even relatively small organizations. But, at the risk of repeating myself, it's not the detail of information that counts, but what you do with it when you've got it.

For most organizations the most sensitive area of the balance sheet and the element that contributes most directly to profit and survival is working capital: how fast you are buying in resources, processing them and then converting them into cash. Consequently, this is the area that I would home in on first, and I would construct my balance sheet report to highlight movements in working capital that were out of line with budget:

- Debtors
- Work in progress
- Stocks
- Creditors
- Cash.

If they are different from expectation, it's time to find out why.

Debtors

Debtors need to be managed by reference to age. You will presumably have a credit policy – payment within 30 days or whatever. You may also have a realistic expectation of how long it takes different classes of debtors to pay. For example, some large companies take full advantage of their size and maximize credit periods at the expense of their suppliers. Whatever the genuinely expected length of payment period, this variable must be managed. Consequently you need to have a clearly laid down policy of what to do if credit periods are breached. The most common argument I hear is 'I can't afford to lose customers by pressing them to pay'. I have a great deal of sympathy with that argument, but on the other hand a customer who doesn't pay or who pays so late as to absorb most of the profit in interest charges is not contributing much to your business. As usual, somewhere in the middle lies the balanced view.

Work in progress

This needs to be managed with reference to the number of days' sales or production you are carrying in this asset category. Project management organizations in particular often suffer problems here. I've encountered organizations that devotedly manage their debtor book but resolutely refuse to manage their work in progress balances. The argument roughly follows the line that they can't force customers to complete a project before they're ready. I think the problem here arises well before you get to the point of creating work in progress. It lies in the failure to lay down proper ground rules for the customer/supplier relationship including frequency of billing and project completion. Look back at the comments in the previous chapter on key performance criteria in project management environments (p. 131). Unless you specify the rules for all aspects of the project that affect your profitability you can expect the customer to take full advantage of your failure to control your business.

Stock

Stock or inventory management is also best undertaken by having a clear idea of how many days' production or turnover you need in stock. That applies both to stock levels overall and to different categories of stock whose costs are material to your profitability. This puts you in a position to manage inventory levels downwards, according to the considerations set out in the last chapter (p. 137).

Creditors

Creditor balances need a management policy as well. Take full advantage of your allowable credit period without ruining supplier relationships by overdoing it. From a management information point of view you need an expectation of the level of trade creditor balances you should be carrying in comparison with the level of business you are doing.

Another point is relevant here. If you're a good payer you put yourself in the 'favoured customer' category with your supplier. From here it should be possible to negotiate all kinds of special arrangements from priority of service to retrospective discounts based on your level of expenditure over a period of time.

This reminds me of a client I had some years ago. Because I was a regular visitor to the company I used to take invoices with me rather than post them. Consistently, as soon as I handed an invoice to the managing director he would reach for his cheque book. Eventually I asked him why he paid so promptly. His answer was simple. He assumed that because he gave me priority I would do the same for him. And when I stopped to think about it, it was true. If there was pressure, it was this account that would always be serviced first. And later in the relationship, when the company needed urgent help, it took only one telephone call to make us move very quickly. Not that we don't move quickly for everyone. Rather, it just seemed as if this was a special relationship that we wanted to do everything possible to maintain. Wouldn't you, with a customer who paid like that? If so, turn it on its head and think about *being* a customer like that.

Cash

Cash management requirements arise in two contexts: those that borrow cash and those that have surplus funds. If you're in the former category, there are two issues. You need to be able to function within your borrowing limits and to manage the cost of money – the interest – which affects your profit levels. Functioning within your borrowing limits implies having a predetermined view of the level of borrowing you will need. This goes back to the issue of budgeting raised above, and then managing the other elements of working capital to ensure you secure the level of cash/overdraft/loan that you expect at a given time. Interest rate management involves the following:

- regularly reviewing your borrowing sources to minimize interest rates;
- being aware that your bank is a supplier in much the same way as your other resource suppliers. The only difference is that this supplier provides you with cash, and wants it back from you at some time. But banks too are driven by the need

to compete and offer as good terms as a borrower of your standing can get elsewhere;

- not taking action that will incur penalties, such as exceeding your overdraft limit or making unscheduled repayments.

If you have surplus funds, you need to manage this resource as effectively as any other. The danger here is that because you're not subject to the outside disciplines that borrowing or external resource purchase imposes, it's much easier to get lazy.

If you have large cash surpluses, you'll have a treasury management function dealing with this for you. Because this department is (presumably) charged with specific responsibility for achieving targets in much the same way as any other department, it faces an equivalent of outside pressure that makes for good discipline.

If your cash surpluses are more humble, it's easy to ignore the issue. In this case the best route is to set targets for what you want your cash to achieve in much the way as you would if you had a department looking after it. The establishment of targets – budgets, if you will – gives you something to aim at. The absence of targets leaves you not really knowing whether you did well or not.

Ratio analysis

Resource management for me implies a need to manage by ratio as well as by absolute level. When all is said and done ratio analysis simply implies managing the relationship between two or more variables. But it does give some crucial additional information on the performance of the business that the absolute figures don't disclose.

When it comes to ratio analysis, it's possible to take this to an almost frightening degree of complexity if you are so minded. Occasionally such complexity may be needed, but I commonly find myself working with the same relatively limited range of ratios when undertaking financial analysis. The following are the ratios I find most useful in assessing the general performance of a business.

Turnover growth

$$\frac{\text{This period's turnover} - \text{last period's turnover}}{\text{Last period's turnover}} \times 100$$

Take this period's (say this year's) turnover, deduct last year's turnover, divide it by last year's turnover and express as a percentage. Now do the same thing over the previous four or five years. What kind of pattern do you see? If you were to apply the same analysis to your key competitors, what would their patterns look like? How would you like it to look next year? How can you achieve this?

Gross profit percentage

$$\frac{\text{Gross profit}}{\text{Turnover}} \times 100$$

Simply divide gross profit by turnover. Now do the same thing for last month . . . and for this month last year. Is it consistent? What is the trend over a period of time? Why is this happening? If you find that you have a consistently rising gross profit percentage, what does this say about your position on the life cycle curve? What implications does that have for the way you're running your business?

Return on capital employed
There are a number of ways of calculating this. I don't think it matters too much which you choose so long as you're consistent. The formula I tend to use is this one:

$$\frac{\text{Profit before interest and tax}}{\text{Shareholders' funds plus long-term debt}}$$

There's some argument over whether you should take profit before or after tax/interest and whether you include or exclude long-term loans. My logic is that businesses have some discretion as to whether they finance themselves with equity or debt. So if I want to find how this business is performing compared with others in the same industry, I should remove the effect of that discretion. I therefore look at the level of return on capital regard-less of the source of that capital.

Of course, this doesn't preclude you from then recalculating to see what return you would get as shareholder with different levels of gearing (debt to equity ratio).

Interest cover
On a related note, any business that borrows significantly should be looking at the level of debt it can safely carry. The most usual way is to consider its interest cover – the number of times it can pay its interest out of profit before interest. It's calculated by:

$$\frac{\text{Profit before interest}}{\text{Interest}}$$

This in its turn raises questions about what level of cover you should be aiming for. I don't think there are any hard and fast rules here. It depends on the degree of confidence you have in the ability of your business to generate profit that will cover interest. There are some industries whose profitability is so volatile that I would feel uncomfortable with budgeted interest cover of less then ten times. There are others whose prospects I am sufficiently confident of that I would tolerate interest cover of only two times – perhaps even less. It depends on your unique circumstances.

Stock turnover
This relates to the points raised above in connection with stock management in general. The point here is that you can monitor the relationship between the level of stock you are carrying and the level of turnover you are achieving. The ratio is given by:

$$\frac{\text{Turnover for the year}}{\text{Stock level}}$$

which gives you the number of times, on average, your stock turns over in the year. That figure has then to be managed. How does your stock turnover compare to competitors'? How has it moved over time? How can you increase it?

Debtor and creditor days

This relates to the overall management of debtors and creditors –
the number of days' sales you have tied up in debtors/creditors.
The ratio can be calculated for each in the same way:

$$\frac{\text{Turnover}}{365 \text{ days}} = \text{average sales per day}$$

$$\frac{\text{Debtors}}{\text{Average sales per day}} = \text{number of days' sales in debtors}$$

Much the same questions then arise: What is the average for the
industry? What policy adjustments are available to you to reduce
the figure?

Break-even point

It's hard to identify any one issue as being the most important in
the financial management of a business, but if there is one I think
this is probably it. If your business faces reasonably consistent
gross profits and overheads, calculating the level of turnover at
which it breaks even is relatively straightforward.

To do this we first need to think in terms of fixed and variable
costs. The former are those costs that you incur that are reasonably consistent regardless of the level of turnover. The latter are
costs that vary in proportion to turnover. A quick and dirty way
of thinking about this is that variable costs often approximate to
cost of sales (i.e. costs before gross profit) and fixed costs approximate to overheads.

It has to be emphasized that this is a generalization, so make
sure it's appropriate to your business before you start to rely on
it. If not, establish which costs are fixed and which variable
before using the following analysis.

Think of break-even in this way:

Turnover	V
Less cost of sales	(W)
Leaves gross profit	X
Less overhead	(Y)
Leaves profit	Z

There is a level of turnover that just covers overhead and leaves no profit at all. This is the break-even level.

If you face overheads of, say, £1,000,000 annually and your gross margin is 40 per cent, break-even turnover is:

$$\frac{\text{Overheads}}{\text{Gross margin}} = \frac{1{,}000{,}000}{0.4} = 2{,}500{,}000$$

Assuming the variables stay consistent, every £1 of turnover you achieve above the £2.5 million mark yields 40p of profit. Conversely every £1 below this figure gives 40p of losses.

This knowledge in itself is needed to make sure you exceed break-even turnover. It's also extremely useful to ask yourself questions about the break-even issue, such as:

● What would happen to break-even turnover (and therefore profitability at all other levels of turnover):

– if you were able to reduce overhead?
– if you were to improve unit gross margin?

● What happens to profitability at existing margin and over-head if you increase turnover by various amounts?
● Which of the three key variables is most subject to your con-trol and what happens if you improve upon it?

Asking questions like these begins to point to the various ways you can influence and manipulate your business to maximize profitability.

Summary

- The most effective way to manage financial performance is to concentrate on summary information and then to home in on areas of detail as needed.
- The control process starts with having a budget, ideally for each level of responsibility or decision-taking within the organization.
- The best budgets are those set on a 'zero basis', i.e. where you re-examine your expectations rather than repeat the previous period's performance or budget.
- Management accounts should ideally disclose summary financial information for key components of both profit and loss accounts and balance sheet.
- The most sensitive elements on the profit and loss account are turnover, margin, overhead and profit. These should be considered in summary form before going on to consider component parts in more detail.
- Key balance sheet items for most organizations are those to do with working capital and liquidity – stocks, work in progress, debtors, creditors and cash. You need to have a clear policy for the management of each of these.
- As well as managing the absolute figures and elements, manage the relationships between them to optimize the performance of your resources.
- Identify the break-even position for your business/operating unit. Consider which variables are most susceptible to your influence and what happens if you begin to alter them.

11 Resource Management Systems – Some Detail

The previous chapter dealt in general with managing the financial performance of your business. As we move down to consider some of the component parts in more detail it's important to emphasize that because the requirements of different businesses are so diverse it's not possible to be comprehensive in the treatment of this content. You may therefore find yourself reading material that doesn't apply to you or wondering at the absence of systems you would expect to see.

However, there are three main systems of detail that we can usefully examine in this context and that should be relevant to almost all businesses:

1 Business generation management
2 Human resource management
3 Quality management.

Business generation management

This is undoubtedly one of the more difficult areas of management, since it involves your interaction with the outside world.

However, as we've noted in Part II, it is possible to control that interaction to some degree, and to deploy your resources intelligently so that you produce the best results. We consistently find that corporate underperformance here relates failure to plan ahead or to think clearly, or to coordinate the resources devoted to business generation.

The following are the considerations that lie at the heart of resource management for business generation:

- What are you seeking to achieve?
- What resources are you likely to require to achieve this target?
- What is the best way of combining the resources?
- What obstacles are likely to get in your way and what can you do about it?

What are you seeking to achieve?

Ultimately, the answer to this question needs to be framed in terms of sales and gross margin targets – now and over a period of time. Typically those targets will be broken into performance units – turnover per product line, per sales outlet, per salesperson and so on. But before you reach the physical target itself you need to have thought about the issues it involves if you want to manage the process properly.

I referred above to the fact that many budgets are set on the basis of satisfying higher management. If that's a good description of how you set a budget, start by at least admitting it to yourself. Go on; no one's looking. Last time you set the budget, were you under time pressure? Did you think of it as just another chore for head office?

Now think about this. What would happen if you also thought about sales targets in terms of the strategic and marketing considerations set out in the first two parts of this book. Suppose for each product, group, outlet, market, you were to take account of strategic considerations of your position on the curve, where the market and competition is going and where you should aim to be going in light of the future and the policies that will take you there?

In most cases you will find that this approach gives rise to a much more sophisticated and logical set of sales targets than if you simply use the basis of last year's figures or how well competitor X is doing this year. Set your targets for individual elements in the sales mix by reference to strategic circumstances rather than habit. After this, everything depends on your unique circumstances.

What resources are you likely to need and how do you combine them?

The resource combinations you will need to achieve your turnover targets will vary from industry to industry. If you're in retail, say, the key elements in your sales mix are likely to include retail space, retail sales staff and particular forms of promotion – point of sale, advertising of various forms etc. If your business is marketing services there's likely to be much more emphasis on face-to-face selling at the customer's premises. The particular mix of resources that works best for your business will be unique to your industry if not to your company.

But don't make the mistake of setting that mix in stone. It takes a zero-based approach to get it right in a changing environment. Whatever industry you're in it's important periodically to go back to basics and ask yourself if you're selling in the most cost-effective way. As prices of resources alter over time and new technology comes on stream the optimal mix of sales resources will also vary.

In years past, you would very probably have used more road sales staff than you do now. In years to come technology will change the cost-effective mix of sales resource. In particular, at the time of writing the Internet is anticipated to change radically the way we all buy and sell. You may even be reading an electronic version of this book. So why haven't you already thought about what's going to happen to the resource mix that will best serve your sales objectives this year, next year and the year after? It's no longer good enough to be part of the field. If you want to succeed you must lead the field at something – and sales needs to be part of that something, whatever you do.

So maybe you have examined resource mix and deployment,

but in my experience most organizations haven't even thought of the overall cost of sales they are facing, let alone considered how to alter the mix to make it more effective. Often it's simply to do with budgets and vested interests. Your marketing manager had a budget last year. He certainly doesn't want it reduced this year, so you continue to promote to much the same extent as you always have. Maybe the promotional mix changes, but not the absolute level.

Your sales director has a team of sales staff. She doesn't want the budget reduced, so you still go on running the same size of sales force that you traditionally have done.

Whose job is it to review the total level of resource you need to achieve your sales targets and the mix of resource you're going to deploy? It must be somebody's job.

What obstacles are likely to get in your way and what can you do about them?

I feel very sad when I see a management team after the end of a year in which they've yet again failed to achieve the targets they set themselves. Of course, sometimes underperformance is universal in an industry. Events take place that no one could have predicted no matter how good their crystal ball. However, more often, some simply succeed and others simply fail. The question may sound harsh, but if someone else in the industry succeeded and you failed, what's your excuse? They did something better than you. Instead of making excuses you need to find out what it was and do even better than them next year if you don't want a repeat performance.

Too many management teams simply accept that others are better than them. I don't subscribe to that view. If it's possible for the competition, it's also possible for you. If they were better organized, better able to predict the future, more flexible or whatever, then it should be possible for you as well. If you choose. And if you commit yourself to finding out what they do that makes the customer want to buy from them.

Having said that, the question is how to stop this happening in the first place. The best solution is to 'forward-think' and anticipate. Consider perpetually what can go wrong that will thwart your objectives and what preventive action you can take before it happens. Dangers creep up on you when you're not looking – so always be on your guard. Be perpetually on the lookout for the next opportunity and the next threat. Be hungry for success or you may never achieve what you're capable of achieving.

Human resource management

It seems to me that the area of human resource management is prone to more double standards than any other aspect of business management. It sometimes appears that those people who write loftily in company reports that 'people are our greatest asset and we must invest in them' are the same ones who write the redundancy notices with often minimal thought given to the human consequences of their actions.

This area of management perhaps needs more clarity than any other: clarity over what is the deal between the organization and the people who work for it: clarity as to what are the respective obligations and rights of each side; and clarity as to what we need from our staff and why they are willing to provide it.

At one level, human resources are not very different from other resources. All resources are engaged in an attempt to achieve corporate goals, usually framed in terms of profit, market share etc. Resources are retained if they continue to contribute actively to the achievement of those objectives. You reorganize and redeploy resources as their relative costs and contributions vary. And in this sense human resources are no different.

Where the difference arises is that here the subject is people. Human beings, not human resources. One of the less pleasant trends of the 1990s has been that some organizations have lost sight of this fact. Others are all too aware of the human consequences of the need to manipulate resources into optimal configurations. They tend to be the ones with the most enlightened staff development programmes and outplacement policies that amount to more than PR.

Nevertheless, profit-making organizations continue to exist

only if they continue to make profit. Those that operate in competitive markets remain competitive only if they, like their competitors, minimize cost. This typically implies the reduction of labour and the increased use of technology.

I believe that this is why the unspoken employment contract has changed so much in the last ten years. Long-term loyalty – regrettably or otherwise – is a thing of the past for most businesses. The deal is now that you hold a position to the extent that, and as long as, you contribute recognizably and measurably to the achievement of the goals of the organization you work for.

But I have a nagging concern that this may be a somewhat short-sighted view. By altering the unspoken contract and changing the basis of motivation from positive to negative it seems to me that you store up problems for the future. Such policies may work in a loose labour market such as that which most of the Western world is facing now, but I question what will happen in the longer term. Very long-run considerations such as demographic change suggest that we may not always face loose labour markets. And when cultural changes such as these have taken place it's hard to see how former relationships based on goodwill can be re-established. It seems to me that what we are tampering with here is the one part of the organization that is capable of innovating. And as argued throughout this book, it may be that the ability to innovate will, in the longer term, represent the only competitive advantage that any organization can sustain (see Chapter 12 for more on this).

Nevertheless, like it or not, it is against a background of largely reducing demand for labour that most organizations are formulating their human resource policies for the rest of the 1990s and the millennium. That being the case, what should a human resources policy look like? What should it do for you?

The general answer is that it should provide you with the volume and quality of resource that you require to achieve your corporate objectives, particularly long-term objectives. That means answering the following questions:

● What are the human resource requirements of the organization implicit in its corporate plan?

- How well does our current human resource base meet the requirements we identify?
- How do we address the gap between the two?
- How do we manage the resource to coordinate goals and activities to achieve the objectives of the organization?

Figure 11.1 shows the steps you need to take to create an effective human resource management system.

What are the human resource requirements of the organization implicit in its corporate plan?

For reasons which are unclear, people are often the resource that is least well coordinated with the organization's plan. Sometimes it's because the organization doesn't have a plan, but others do and still don't coordinate their human resource policies with it. If you follow the corporate plan through to its logical conclusion you should be able to identify what numbers of people you will require to achieve your objectives, at what levels, with what skills, where they should be and so on.

You should also plan for a range of scenarios: what you'll need if you do achieve performance target and growth rate; what you'll need if you fall short of target to various degrees; what you'll need if you exceed budget. And then think about how you will create the flexibility needed to address each of these scenarios.

How well does our current human resource base meet the requirements we identify?

The next step in successfully managing the resource to the achievement of the outcome is to identify your current human resources and assess how well they meet your needs. This should be done for each facet you identified as significant at the previous stage – numbers, skills, locations, levels and so on. This 'human resource audit,' as it's commonly known, should incorporate a development or training needs analysis.

How do we address the gap between the two?

When you know what the gap is you can develop a plan for

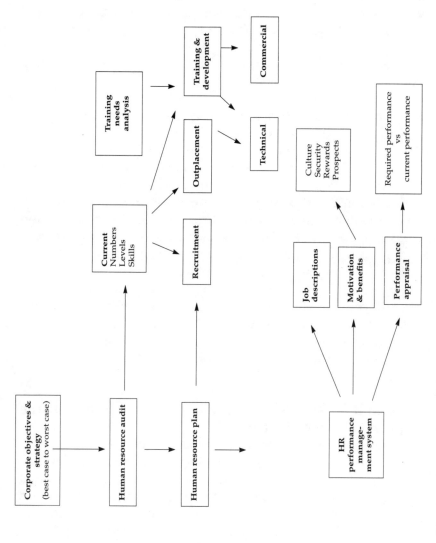

Figure 11.1   Human resource management system

closing it: by recruitment, development and training and, if necessary, outplacement (please be sensitive here).

How do we manage the resource to coordinate goals and activities to achieve the objectives of the organization?

If I am a member of the staff and you want to get the best out of me, you should ensure that a certain structure underpins our relationship:

- I need to know what the job is – an objective job description is a 'need to have', not a 'nice to have'.
- I need to have the personal capacity for it – physically, emotionally and intellectually. This is an issue of selection interviewing, training or both.
- I need to know your performance expectations of me in this role, i.e. what objectives you want me to achieve.
- I need to be motivated, usually by a combination of organizational culture, security, rewards and prospects for the future. In this context you should take particular account of the messages that I receive from both the tangible and intangible reward systems. You get the behaviour that you encourage. So precisely what type of behaviour does your reward system and culture encourage?
- I need feedback on how well you think I am doing, and an opportunity to provide you with feedback on any impediments the organization is placing on my performance and on what you can do to help me improve – a performance appraisal system.

If any of these elements is missing or indifferently applied, the performance of your human resource will be below capacity.

It should be very clear by now that behind each of these issues lies a great deal of thinking and work for someone in the organization – you, a designated manager or the personnel department. And if it's either of the last two, be aware of the risk that delegation can diminish the seriousness with which the issue is treated. This is one factor that you certainly cannot afford to undervalue, so think very carefully about the delegation process and make sure your organization gets it right.

Quality management

I raise the issue of quality management systems here, not because I want to detail what the features of a quality management system should be – there's already enough literature to fill a library on that subject – but because I believe that thinking on quality management has been somewhat 'off-beam' over the last few years. And from this assertion it is but one small step to advocating that if you want quality management to be effective, you need to be clear about what you want from it.

In Western industrialized society the 1980s and 1990s have seen an increasing consciousness of the quality issue, and a considerable industry has grown up on the back of it. Meanwhile, other business cultures, notably the Japanese, have looked on somewhat bemused, wondering why you need a complex system of near religious status to do something as obvious as get your job right first time.

Perhaps I'm being a bit unfair here; Western producers certainly needed something to shake them out of their complacency. But I do find myself wondering to what extent we've lost sight of the objective of quality management by concentrating so much on the process.

So why do you need a quality management system?

You'd think it would be everyone's first question wouldn't you? However, my experience is that many of the organizations that go down the quality lane don't give this question much thought.

A quality system is often driven by customer requirement. 'If you haven't got ISO 9000 you don't work for us' is quite a powerful argument. Even more common is a sense of unease among those that initiate the creation of such a system, as if something's happening that you should be a part of. You're not quite sure why; it's just that everyone else seems to be doing it and you don't want to be left behind.

Let's ask that fundamental question: Why *do* you want a quality management system? I can see two categories of legitimate answers to this: those that are market-driven and those that involve a genuine concern with the quality of output. If the former, at least be clear about the reasons for doing it. If the latter, the issue should revolve around the question 'How can we be sure that we deliver quality and value in the customer's eyes?'

From here we can presumably conclude that you're dissatisfied with the quality of your output in some sense. And that in turn implies that you have some (I hope objective) standard for judging the quality of what you do. If it's neither, think very carefully about what you expect this supposed panacea to do for you.

Assuming you need a system, what should it be seeking to achieve?

This is a question I prefer to answer in the context of individual circumstances. After all, if your internal inefficiencies are costing you 25 per cent of turnover, your feasible objectives are going to be different from those if they're costing you 5 per cent of turnover.

Hence the first step is to make some reasoned estimate of what quality costs or 'costs of non-conformance' (CONC) amount to in your organization. For example, you are traditionally advised to include here the cost of aborted work (taking into account the stage of added value it has reached in your production process), the cost of reworking and the cost of collection from customer site if the product has actually been delivered. But there are other items I'd want to take account of here as well. How much has it cost you to be out of stock when a customer has asked for something? How much has it cost you to be holding excessive stocks because you're not planning effectively or because you have to plan for errors? How much does the loss of customer goodwill cost you when you get something wrong, or what does it cost to compensate the customer in order to preserve the relationship?

I suggest that in the long run it's cheaper to get things right first time, even though doing so may require the creation of a system and a cultural change incurring expenditure. Now, to my mind, *that's* the reason that you need a system for managing quality in the organization.

If this is so, you need very deliberately to dispense with all the razzmatazz that's currently surrounding the subject and concentrate on outcomes. If the outcome is reduced CONC, specifically what are you aiming for and how will you know when you've got it? What tangible costs savings will accrue? What will you individually and the organization corporately see, hear and do differently from the way things are now? Without this clear representation of your objective you can't hope to achieve what serious quality control is capable of delivering.

So how do you install ISO 9000?
Allowing for variations in individual circumstances, the overriding answer must be 'as cost-effectively as possible'. To stand any chance of working it must have commitment by the organization from chief executive downwards. It must be a project, managed as any other project would be. That means deadline, quality and cost management, the devotion of resource and the measurement of achievement. And as with any other project, you need to ensure that the quality of resource you devote is capable of delivering the results you are looking for. If you don't have competence in-house, you need to draft it in or train it in.

And when you've got it?
The piece of paper finally arrives. You frame it and hang it in the reception area. You put the logo on your stationery. But business doesn't flood in? And the system only prevents delivery of non-conforming product to the customer? It doesn't stop things going wrong in the first place?

You need to realize two things. From a marketing point of view you have at best created a distinctive competence, not a marketing tool (see Part II above). From here you need to transform the ore of distinctive competence into the scythe of marketing communication that will cut effectively into the marketplace. And even then you need to realize that you might simply steal a temporary march on the competition or, even worse, only catch up.

From an internal point of view you need to bring about cultural changes in the organization that result in people *wanting* to get it right first time and then ensure the system permits and encourages them to do so. And that's much more complicated, involving leadership and motivation (see Chapter 12 below).

Summary

- Effective resource management depends first and foremost on having clear objectives for the resource you are deploying.
- In business generation you need to deploy a balanced combination of human and non-human resources. What is effective will vary considerably over time. You need to build flexibility into your thinking and systems or you will get stuck with a broadly similar combination year after year, which will result in diminishing market share.
- Where you underperform by comparison with your objectives or by comparison with others, you need to treat that underperformance as feedback, not failure. There are lessons to learn here about the way you are doing things and how you could be doing them to get better results. Learn, implement and improve.
- Human resource management requires considerable flexibility (which is market-driven) and extreme sensitivity (which, in my opinion, should be morally driven).
- You need to recognize that the unspoken employment contract has changed and people relate to their organizations differently now from how they used to.
- The policies you deploy now will determine the culture and reputation of the organization, and your human interactions for many years to come. Be clear about the kind of organization you want to be ten or even twenty years hence before locking into a human resources policy.
- Make sure that your human resource policy is coordinated with your corporate objectives and is run by reference to a clearly understood system. People need to know the rules of the game and should not have to second-guess you if you want to get the best out of them.

- Enter into the quality management arena only when you are clear about what you want from the process. Expect measurable results; find out, if you're not getting them, why not.
- When you have the system, recognize that you're just starting, not finishing. Achieving deliverable results from a quality management system has more to do with cultural and attitudinal change than with system change.

12 Management Management Systems

Part III has been focusing on the way you can control the internal workings of the organization with a view to maximizing profit. Chapter 9 dealt specifically with managing the productive process and the last two chapters have examined the various control systems you should have in place, in general and in detail, if you want the business to achieve what it is capable of achieving. In this final chapter we turn to the subject of management itself – last not because it is the least important, but because it is perhaps the most important.

The control of the processes outlined in Chapters 10 and 11 is a management function – the deployment of resources in the most efficient way to achieve given objectives. But in addition to having systems for controlling the various parts of the business, the process of management is itself susceptible to objective analysis and systematization. The result of taking this approach should be to make management itself more effective. Therefore, this final chapter deals with the process of management itself – the means by which we pull everything else in the organization together.

The main thesis of this book has been that it is clarity of

thought and understanding that delivers the ability to maximize profit. And that clarity is at least as necessary in the area that we call management as anywhere else. There are four areas we need to tackle.

- *What are you trying to achieve through management?* This has to do with being clear about what you are trying to achieve – through mission statements and business plans and through communication of your plans to all those that will play a part in their achievement.
- *Is the organization formally structured in a way that supports your management objectives?* Have you structured the organization in a manner that is conducive to the achievement of its objectives?
- *Is the process of management working effectively?* Are you leading the organization so as to coordinate its activities and efforts with the achievement of its objectives?
- *Is the concept of change built into the system of management?* Are you monitoring your management system and its achievements? Are you innovating perpetually to ensure its objectives remain dynamic in the context of an external environment that is for ever changing?

Missions and business plans

Ask yourself what you want out of your business. In some cases the answers will be very well established. Larger public companies will often have clear expectations placed upon them as to share prices, growth rates and PE ratios. Smaller organizations will often have a less clear outcome in mind. But sometimes, so will very large ones. It's been interesting to note over the last few years the number of very large entities that have been considering or actually repaying cash to shareholders, apparently because they can't think of anything better to do with it! This suggests something lacking at the highest levels of objective-setting in the business.

I think it's legitimate to think first and foremost about what you are seeking to achieve by being in business, a question that should be answered both personally and corporately. The extent to which your own personal outcomes converge with organizational objectives determines whether you will be able to act consistently with those objectives. The psychologists refer to this as 'goal congruence' and I think it's one of the most significant factors in organizational achievement (see 'Leadership and Motivation' below for more).

At personal level, you need to ask yourself to what extent the business, or your role within it, is an expression of who you are or want to be. The most successful business managers and proprietors – and any job-holders for that matter – are those who have a genuine commitment to what they do. An ability to give of yourself to the customer (be that a purchaser or simply someone else in the organization) makes an immeasurable difference to the quality of what you provide. By contrast, the grudging giver whose heart is not in the job and who measures out exactly that to which I am entitled and no more is not someone I would choose to do business with if there were an alternative.

At the corporate level being clear about objectives can be complex. Nevertheless, it is necessary; if you want everyone else in the organization to behave sympathetically with the organization's goals there must be a clear understanding throughout the business of what those goals are. Hence the need for a mission and business plan.

In simple terms, the mission statement exists to express the purpose of the organization ('It is the purpose of Sticky Fings Limited to supply the best toffee apples available anywhere in North Korea'). The business plan exists to set out how you will achieve your mission and will typically have a number of identifiable component parts:

1   Objectives:
    ● to sell $10 million of toffee apples next year at 5 per cent gross margin;
    ● to achieve 30 per cent of the North Korean toffee apple market by 2200 AD.

2   Strategy:
  ● penetration of the North Korean market will be achieved by a combination of Internet advertising and rickshaw hoardings.
3   Action plan:
  ● buy a modem to facilitate Internet advertising;
  ● negotiate rickshaw advertising rates.
4   Monitoring:
  ● monthly board meetings to monitor the sales effects of rickshaw hoardings.

The business plan will usually be arrived at after investigation of current performance, market opportunity and feasible objectives. Once available, you need to live by it, evolve it in line with perpetually changing environmental conditions and monitor your progress towards your agreed stated aims.

You then face the issue of how much of it should be disclosed to the rest of the organization without running the risk of divulging commercially sensitive information. There's very little point in creating a corporate plan unless those who are to participate in its achievement and will feel its effects have a good working knowledge of what's expected of them and why. For reasons of commercial confidentiality the contents will not be available to all and sundry, but you must let your staff have enough information to behave in keeping with the business's objectives.

Organizational structure

I can't tell you what your organizational structure should look like. Its size and shape will be intrinsic to the scale and nature of your business. But we can say with some confidence that a properly conceived business plan will point towards an organizational structure that will be optimal in achieving its objectives. Compare your present structure with the objectives of the plan and ask yourself what each element in the structure is delivering towards the achievement of the business's objectives. Too often individual job functions and even whole departments are a hangover from how things used to be years ago and are no longer relevant to the present aims of the business. The current fashionable term for this is 'Business process re-engineering' and you can be charged a great deal of money for it. I think that forward-looking market-oriented organizations have been doing it for ever anyway.

The most common problem that we encounter in connection with organizational structures is those businesses (and I would actually number them as the majority) that have structures built around the people that work for the company rather than around the requirements of the business. This phenomenon is more widespread among smaller organizations (but also sometimes visible within departments of larger companies), and tends to occur as business grows. To start with there's yourself, Fred and Mabel, so you naturally divide the work between yourselves. Ten years later you, Fred and Mabel, have each got 200 people in your departments and the work is still structured in much the same way. It's easy to see how it happens. You've concentrated so much on building the volume of the business that you've lost sight of its structure. And you can't bring yourself to reward loyal staff with demotion or outplacement, even if, as is often the case, the people that coped well in a small company are floundering expensively in a much larger one.

Nevertheless, to avoid this you should periodically reassess the organizational structure that the business requires. Everyone should be aware from day one that it is the needs of the business that define the shape of the organization, not personal preference for particular ways of working.

One good example of what happens when you don't structure the organization in line with its objectives is the case of company K with which we worked some time ago. We had been appointed at the request of an institutional investor in company K to find out why the organization was failing to meet its profit targets. Company K had been formed some two years previously by the merger of two other organizations.

Now, from the individual's point of view, merger can be one of the most harrowing processes that you can undergo, simply because most people in the organization do not know what to expect. You're aware that everything can change. It's possible that your job may cease to exist; you have no idea what the other side's people are like and so on. Cultural change is inevitable but you don't know what it's going to amount to.

Company K had all of these characteristics and many more. Two structures had been brought together into one and put down on a single, rather large site. The boards of directors had been merged (creating a very large and singularly unwieldy structure). All directors of both companies remained on the board. The sales functions of the two companies had been merged – but little thought had been given to allocation of territories and reporting methods, with the result that the sales force was demotivated. The production methodologies were largely incompatible – so they were all kept and run semi-independently.

All this had happened because the focus of the merger had been low level and short term, with very little thought given to high-level and long-term issues. The solution to this, among a whole range of other issues that needed to be addressed, was to go back to the basic question of what the business was expected to achieve. From there it was possible to ask what resources were needed and in what combinations. At that point we were able to identify the ways in which the structure failed to support the outcomes the company was seeking and we could offer suggestions accordingly.

Leadership and motivation

We first touched on the subject of motivation in the context of sales, in the last section of Chapter 6, 'The final issue'. Here I want to consider the wider issue of motivation through the rest of the company. How do you know when you are managing effectively? I can think of only one answer: you are achieving your objectives. You can put a rider on it if you wish and say that you're achieving your objectives through the minimum use of resources, but the answer is at root the same.

The key issue here is that in most cases you will be addressing those objectives in concert with others. Whether you run a small company, lead a department in a large organization, or whether you're responsible for the whole of a large business, to a great extent you will be as successful as your ability to communicate, to motivate and to mobilize the efforts of others in pursuit of clearly defined corporate goals.

Enough has been written on the subject of motivation and leadership to fill many libraries, so the contribution we shall make here is limited to the general view of how it fits in to the running of the business. The intention of this book is to help you see the big issues from far enough away for them to make sense, and then enable you to focus back in detail on how these issues relate to your own circumstances. The following questions must be answered in relation to motivation:

Are you getting what you want – in management?

Leadership and motivation take place in the context of personal and corporate objectives. If you're realizing those objectives and are confident that you will continue to do so, don't change until the need arises. Be wary of this year's fashionable management theory, whether it be TQM, business process re-engineering or whatever. Change for change's sake is expensive and doesn't necessarily yield better results than before.

On the other hand, if you're not getting what you want it is time to make some changes. But take care over this; be certain to:

- identify what you want but are failing to achieve;
- identify why you're not achieving it;
- make the change at the point of breakdown.

The point of breakdown is a subject in itself. It can be a specific structural factor in the management system (say lack of a staff feedback mechanism causing mounting frustration). Equally, it may be to do with human underperformance – perhaps a manager who simply has no idea of how to motivate and lead others. Or it could be a cultural/philosophical issue, such as an implicit corporate belief that people do not matter.

If you've followed the reasoning of this book so far, I'm

hopeful that you've developed a perspective that enables you to identify the aspects of your activities that are not yet delivering the results you are looking for. If you're still not quite there, start at the highest category level and let your thinking cascade downwards. Is the problem in the external environment, the communication process or in internal organization? When you've identified that, move on down to the next level. Use Figure 12.1 to help you.

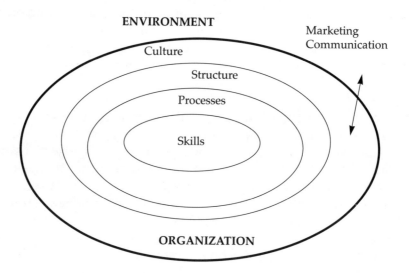

Figure 12.1   Identifying sources of motivational breakdown

The biggest failure of management may be in attempting to solve the perceived problem without recognizing the true problem.

Are your staff getting what they want?

We touched earlier on the subject of goal congruence. The argument here is that if everyone wants something different they will tend to pull in all sorts of different directions to get it. The clever bit is to motivate the staff by hitching their objectives to the organization's. Bear in mind that each individual is motivated by his/her unique factors.

How are you motivated?

What are the consequences of your personal motivational style? Your style will consist of a range of factors that trigger your response. The biggest mistake we see managers making is to assume that everyone else is motivated by the same factors that they themselves find motivating. The key to motivating another individual effectively is to identify their personal triggers and manage with those in mind rather than your own.

There are as many motivators as there are people – and then to the factor of ten. But there are groups of factors that are common to many people. Finding the right issues for the right people starts with identifying their personal tendencies. Take a particular individual as case in point and then ask yourself the following questions.

Do they tend to be more motivated by:

- *Moving towards things they want or away from things they don't want*? For example, did they buy the new car more for the prestige of owning the new vehicle or more because of the fear of the old one breaking down?
- *The necessity or the possibilities of doing things*? Are obligations and responsibilities more important to them or interest, opportunities and potential?
- Interest in *themselves* or *in others*? Are they more concerned with green issues, the Third World, wanting to do good in society, or is the WIIFM factor (what's in it for me?) the crucial ingredient?
- *The big picture or the small picture*? Do they tend to focus on the overall general shape and structure of a situation or do they concentrate more on detail? Is organizing the village fête more about marketing programmes and socioeconomic trends or making sure the tickets for the tombola are the right colour?

There are many possible pairs of variables, but the above are some of the more common ones we come across.

That quality of information about a given individual (or a whole corporate culture) is mainly gained through paying attention, and it puts you in a far stronger position to motivate. This is simply because you can express yourself, not in terms that would appeal to you, but in terms that the particular individual will find appealing.

The concept of 'more or less motivated' is important here. Most people have a mixture of both factors in each case (if the variable is important to them at all) but they tend towards one side or the other.

What one feature could you change that would make the most significant difference to your management performance?

Stop and think for a moment. Put the book down and ask yourself this question. Give yourself no more than 30 seconds to answer. If you could only change one feature of your management and leadership style that would make an overriding difference to your results, what would it be? Write it down before you forget it. What difference would it make? How would you know the change was effective and lasting? And finally, so what's stopping you from doing it?

Innovation

In a sense the whole of this book has been about innovation. At the most basic level of running a business you have only two choices. You can either go on doing what you're doing or you can do it differently. The only justification for doing it differently is that you want to get different results – now or in the future.

The reason that innovation is so very important is that everything around you is changing, and will continue to change. And in most environments an arithmetical rate of change has given way to a geometric rate of change, which is in turn giving way to an exponential rate of change. It seems that the expectation of change is the one and only feature of life that is constant. Change is here to stay.

Are you going to see this fact as positive or negative? As an opportunity or a threat? Your perspective on change will determine how you react to it and how far you are able to turn it to your advantage. The whole process of business can ultimately be viewed as one huge opportunity for the benefit of the organization and the customer alike. But customer needs are dynamic and you too must be always moving on.

Furthermore, it used to be sufficient to follow change. At the forefront of innovation would be a few market leaders and the rest of us would catch up eventually. We were content to be followers. But markets respond to change. It's only by offering something better or cheaper that you stay in business now, so you can no longer afford to lag behind the market leaders. The focus of what you do today must be the effect it will have tomorrow.

Technology and culture make change both possible and essential. Consumer products reaching the market are said to have a lead over the competition of an average of six months. That's all it takes for the rest of the pack to catch up and leapfrog.

You must therefore continue to innovate, delivering more advantage to your customer in what you offer and the way you produce and provide it, reflected in the prices you charge. After you've begun to deal with all the other issues this book has raised for you, just reflect on one question. If you can make all these changes in your business today, what will you do tomorrow to stay at the leading edge of what you do?

Whatever it is, all the best with it.

Summary

- Management is itself a process that is susceptible to improved analysis and increased effectiveness. You achieve this through being clear about your objectives, ensuring your structures and processes of management are supporting them and ensuring the concept of change is built into them.
- Clarity about objectives is both a personal and corporate issue. If you know what you want you are in a better position to put more of yourself into what you do.
- Corporate clarification can best be achieved by the development of missions and business plans and their dissemination to those who effect their outcomes.

- The structure you adopt for your organization can be optimal or sub-optimal in terms of the support it lends to the achievement of your objectives. Structure the organization more for the objectives than for the preferences of the people who work for it.
- The process of management requires the effort of many. Leadership and motivation of those concerned needs to be on their terms, not yours. Find the motivational triggers for other people, and remember they may be different from yours.
- Finally, make innovation and constant added value a key value in your organization. You simply cannot afford to ignore it.

A personal message from the author

So now you've come to the end of *How to Make More Profit*. But before we close, take a look back at the introduction. There I told you that this book represents a model based on the distilled experience of over three hundred companies. If you apply it, it can make the difference between mediocrity and dramatic success in your business.

So your next step needs to be to decide how to apply it to your own circumstances.

Maybe you know already what you will do, maybe not. Either way I'd like you to know that I've helped many clients and readers of earlier books to achieve their objectives in business through my management consultancy practice, Winsors. If you could use some help identifying how to improve performance or implementing solutions in your business, I invite you to call me. I look forward to hearing from you.

Yours sincerely

Michael Lawson

WINSORS
MANAGEMENT CONSULTANTS

Telephone: United Kingdom

07000 780188

Winsors Management Consultants Ltd
48 Link Side
Enfield
Middlesex
EN2 7QU
UK

Index